CONGRESS

CONGRESS
THE ELECTORAL CONNECTION

Second Edition

David R. Mayhew

Foreword by R. Douglas Arnold

New Haven and London, Yale University Press

Originally published with assistance from the foundation established in memory of Philip William McMillan of the Class of 1894, Yale College.

First published 1974 by Yale University Press.
Second Edition published 2004 by Yale University Press.

Printed in the United States of America

Library of Congress Control Number: 2004110395
ISBN 0-300-10587-8 (pbk. : alk. paper)

A catalogue record for this book is available from the British Library.

The paper in this book meets the guidelines for permanence and durability of the Committee on Production Guidelines for Book Longevity of the Council on Library Resources.

10 9 8 7 6 5 4 3 2 1

CONTENTS

Foreword by R. Douglas Arnold   vii

Preface to the Second Edition   xiii

Acknowledgments   xxi

Introduction   1

1 The Electoral Incentive   11

2 Processes and Policies   79

Index   181

FOREWORD BY
R. DOUGLAS ARNOLD

Thirty years ago this short book revolutionized the study of Congress. The congressional literature was already large and illuminating. Postwar scholars using a variety of research methods, including case studies, participant observation, and quantitative analysis, had done important work on every aspect of congressional behavior. We knew about elections, careers, committees, parties, state delegations, leaders, seniority, rules, roll calls, and policymaking. A decade later the literature was on a new path — more theoretical and more rigorous; three decades later the literature was transformed. These shifts were partly a consequence of this elegant book.

What made David Mayhew's book so influential? First, it was the initial attempt to integrate what we knew about Congress with a simple, parsimonious theory. Mayhew's theory was the political science equivalent of plate tectonics theory, which had revolutionized geology in the previous decade. Both theories attempted to explain a wide range of outcomes from a single assumption. Plate tectonics theorists assumed that the earth's outer shell was composed of a dozen or so large plates and argued that the plates' movements and collisions explained earthquakes, volcanoes, mountain ranges, continental shapes, ocean ridges, and the worldwide distribution of species. Mayhew assumed that legislators were single-minded seekers of reelection and showed how the pursuit of this goal affected the way legislators allocated time, sought publicity, took positions, organized Congress, interacted with each other, dealt with interest groups, and made public policy. It helped, of course, that most congressional scholars found his arguments persuasive. He was not challenging what we knew; he was arguing that much of what we knew was caused by a single force—legislators' incessant quest for reelection.

Second, the time was ripe for a rational choice explanation of legislative behavior. Although rational choice theory was making inroads into political science, it was not yet firmly established. Two economists had shown the way—Anthony Downs for political parties (1957) and Mancur Olson for interest groups (1965). But no one had attempted a comprehensive rational choice explanation for any of the major governmental institutions: legislatures, executives, courts, or bureaucracies. Mayhew crafted a theory that was every bit as original as what Downs and Olson had created. Unlike the two economists, however, he had first-hand knowledge of his subject—he had spent a year on Capitol Hill—and an encyclopedic knowledge of the congressional literature. He was

able to buttress his arguments with well-chosen examples from the real world and with extensive citations
to empirical studies. It also helped that Mayhew was
theorizing about the calculating behavior of full-time
politicians. In retrospect, it is clear that rational
choice theory is vastly more successful explaining the
behavior of elites (legislators, executives, bureaucrats), whose careers are at stake, than explaining the
behavior of ordinary citizens, who are deciding about
matters less central to their lives, like how to vote or
whether to join an interest group.

Finally, Mayhew was not alone in his embrace of
rational choice theory. The year before, Richard
Fenno, the discipline's most distinguished legislative
scholar, adopted a rational choice approach in his
book comparing congressional committees (1973).
After interviewing more than two hundred members
of six House committees, Fenno concluded that
members pursued three principal goals — reelection,
influence within the House, and good public policy.
Legislators who were strongly motivated by a single
goal tended to join the same committees and structure those committees to achieve their common goal.
The parsimonious Mayhew and the nuanced Fenno
provided alternative models for constructing rational
choice theories about Congress. They also demonstrated the virtue of combining theoretical and empirical analyses.

Rational choice theory is now the dominant theoretical approach for explaining congressional organi-

zation and behavior. Although all scholars do not
begin with the same assumption about legislators'
goals, their style of reasoning is similar. Rational
choice theory has proven itself remarkably versatile
for studying congressional history, organization, committees, rules, reform, budgeting, policymaking, and
the relations between legislators and various political
actors, including bureaucrats, presidents, and interest groups. Even those who do not share Mayhew's
view that political parties are not the centerpiece of
congressional politics use rational choice theory to
advance their arguments.

A very different consequence was to invigorate the
study of congressional elections. If the electoral connection was central to understanding Congress, then
we needed a better understanding of what accounts
for incumbents' repeated success at the ballot box.
The view at the time was that congressional elections
were largely partisan contests. Voters knew so little
about the candidates that the best they could do was
to vote based on party identification or on the economic performance of the incumbent party. Mayhew
undermined that notion in this book and demolished
it in a companion article, published the same year,
"The Case of the Vanishing Marginals." These two
works sparked an explosion of interest in congressional elections. The literature on congressional elections, once a backwater, is now one of the most distinguished literatures in American politics.

Finally, Mayhew gave us the vocabulary to discuss

political accountability. American scholars had long been prisoners of the doctrine of responsible party government. According to the tenets of that creed, (a) strong parties were necessary for voters to hold politicians accountable, (b) the United States did not have strong parties, and, therefore, (c) citizens could not hold politicians accountable for governmental actions. Mayhew urged us to examine what individual candidates do to attain office, what incumbent legislators do to retain office, and how voters decide among competing candidates. By focusing on the behavior of individual voters and legislators he gave us the tools to analyze political accountability in the American setting. Moreover, he identified the key accountability problem in American politics. The electoral connection guarantees that legislators take pleasing positions, but it does nothing to impel legislators to produce pleasing effects.

How has the book stood the test of time? Any thirty-year-old book in political science faces two challenges. The world can change, and scholars can discover new things about the way the world operates. Well, the world has changed. If Mayhew were writing today he would need to address additional questions. Why did the House adopt centralizing reforms? How has the relentless pursuit of campaign funds affected legislators' behavior? Why does zero-sum conflict occur more frequently? Are party leaders more influential? Although the world has changed, the fundamental logic that Mayhew identified is still the dominant force in the American Congress. Candidates still decide when and where to run for office; they still assemble their own electoral coalitions; they still survive in office only as long as they please their constituents. Knowing these three things gives one enormous leverage in understanding the behavior of individual legislators in Congress. Some people believe that political parties are now fundamentally important for understanding congressional behavior. Perhaps they are. Nevertheless, the crucial question is how legislators make the tradeoff between party and constituency. In the world I observe, most legislators would rather offend party leaders or the president than offend their reelection constituency. That is the essence of legislative politics, Washington style.

PREFACE TO THE
SECOND EDITION

I have not tried to revise or update this 1974 work. That would be a nightmarish task given the outpouring of political experience and congressional scholarship during the past thirty years.[1] I hope the original version still has value as a theoretical enterprise, or at least as a kind of theoretical enterprise. After thirty years, I do have five observations that might interest an old or new reader.[2] The first two address the question: What kind of work is this? The following three ask: How have I come to think of this book in light of subsequent events and scholarship?

What Kind of Work Is This Book?

First, as any reader will discover, the book is a theoretical work that obviously goes too far. It is an inten-

---

1. For a newer theoretical treatment, see R. Douglas Arnold, *The Logic of Congressional Action* (New Haven: Yale University Press, 1990).
2. Much of the following material appeared in David R. Mayhew, "Observations on *Congress: The Electoral Connection* a Quarter Century After Writing It," *PS: Political Science and Politics* 34 (2001), 251–52.

tional caricature. I planned the book that way on the assumption that advancing a simple argument to its limits might have explanatory utility. I realized in 1974, as I do now, that political reality is complicated, that no one kind of politician's move can explain everything, and that moves other than ones pointing to an electoral incentive can also have considerable utility. I have been exploring another kind of move in recent work.[3] But in the mid-1970s I was taken by the idea of using the electoral incentive as an explanatory lever. *The Electoral Connection* had a clear origin. One day I was preparing to teach Anthony Downs's *Economic Theory of Democracy* in a graduate seminar, and I toyed with the idea of relaxing Downs's assumption of point-source parties to accommodate the sorts of electoral incentives impinging on individual members of Congress.[4] That led on the spot to a central distinction I draw in *The Electoral Connection* between "credit claiming" and "position taking" — a complication of Downs, but still a caricature.

Second, the book is empirically driven as well as theoretical. Absent my experience as an American Political Science Association Congressional Fellow in 1967–68, there is not the slightest chance that I would have conceived or written *The Electoral Connection*. Be-

3. David R. Mayhew, *America's Congress: Actions in the Public Sphere, James Madison Through Newt Gingrich* (New Haven: Yale University Press, 2000).

4. Anthony Downs, *An Economic Theory of Democracy* (New York: Harper and Row, 1957).

fore those years I had pored over the relevant scholarship, but I did not know the congressional context or possess the confidence to write about it. The book is largely a sketch of what I thought I saw on Capitol Hill. In general, I believe that seeing is a good preface or accompaniment to theorizing.

How Do I Think of the Book Now?

Third, to switch to developments since 1974, the book's idea of credit claiming has received ample notice, but I have been somewhat disappointed by the academic community's reception to position taking. I remain convinced that politicians often get rewarded for taking positions rather than achieving effects. This happens a great deal. One key result is that popular, as opposed to scientific, conceptions of cause and effect often become embodied in lawmaking processes and laws. It may look good back home to favor "gun control" or "saving Social Security" even though laws bearing those labels might not amount to much according to strict standards of instrumental rationality. Endeavors like establishing a "patient's bill of rights" and "repealing the death tax" have large helpings of spin. Congress is not a research bureau, and as long as electoral incentives keep impinging on individual members it is not likely to come to resemble one. In regard to position taking, note also that that impulse limits the degree to which members of Congress are likely to engage in strategic behavior in roll-call voting. A member needs to take defensible positions all the time, not just on a bill's final passage. This is an idea I have not seen expressed very often. In general, my guess is that position taking has not been examined thoroughly since 1974 because its importance exceeds its modelability. And if it implicates causal relations it is especially tough to address.

Fourth, *The Electoral Connection* is often read to say that members are animated to cater *directly* to their home-district voters by supporting pork-barrel projects, taking feel-good positions, tracing lost Social Security checks, and the like, and that that's the whole story. There are no intermediaries. But I presented a somewhat different argument: "What a congressman has to do is to insure that in primary and general elections the resource balance (with all other deployed resources finally translated into votes) favors himself rather than somebody else" (p. 43). That entails catering to relevant political actors, defined as "anyone who has a resource that might be used in the election in question. At the ballot box the only usable resources are votes, but there are resources that can be translated into votes: money, the ability to make persuasive endorsements, organizational skills, and so on" (p. 39). This is not a minor distinction. For example, if I were recrafting *The Electoral Connection* today, I would probably make more out of members' campaign finance networks as collections of "relevant political actors." That would be true to the 1974 definitional language. Today a member may need to cater to a cross-country finance constituency in order to keep scoring with a home-district voter constituency. Southern Democrats running for the Senate, for example, seem to need to raise money in Hollywood. It is a dual-constituency pattern. Also on the campaign finance front, an incumbent may stock up enough campaign money to scare off strong challengers. That is a perfect instance of acting so as to influence relevant political actors, even if home-district voters know nothing about it.

Fifth, let me admit that if I were writing *The Electoral Connection* today I would back off from claiming that "no theoretical treatment of the United States Congress that posits parties as analytic units will go very far" (p. 27). From the perspective of 2004 it is easy to see that the congressional parties bottomed out in importance around 1970 and that they have grown considerably more important in various ways since that time. That much is clear. Still, I have not seen any evidence that today's congressional party leaders "whip" or "pressure" their members more frequently or effectively than did their predecessors thirty years ago. Instead, today's pattern of high roll-call loyalty seems to owe a debt to a post-1960s increase in each party's "natural" ideological homogeneity across its universe of home constituencies. Somehow, the causation lurks down there in the states and districts.[5]

5. See Jon R. Bond and Richard Fleisher, "The Disappearance of Moderate and Cross-Pressured Members of Congress: Conversion, Replacement and Electoral Change," paper pre-

Also, even in an era of stronger party leadership and high party loyalty, there are limits. A key finding of recent research is that members of a House majority party can profit individually in the next election through what might be called "centrist defecting" — that is, by voting with the minority party on roll calls where their own party's stance is risky back home. Perhaps we all knew this, but I had not seen the effect measured in sophisticated fashion until recently. The phenomenon has been observed on roll calls on showdown budgetary questions in general during the 1980s and 1990s, on three major White House or Democratic measures during 1993–94 — Clinton's budget package of 1993, the North American Free Trade Agreement (NAFTA), and the party's omnibus crime measure of 1994 — and on the Republicans' Contract with America in 1995.[6]

---

sented at the annual meeting of the American Political Science Association, San Francisco, 2001. For a state-of-the-art treatment of the relationship between constituencies and roll-call voting, see James M. Snyder, Jr., and Michael Ting, "Roll Calls, Party Labels, and Elections," *Political Analysis* 11 (2003), 419–44.

6. On budgets: Gary C. Jacobson and Gregory L. Bovitz, "The Electoral Politics of Budgets and Deficits, 1980–1996," paper presented at the annual meeting of the American Political Science Association, Boston, 1998. On the Democratic measures: Gary C. Jacobson, "The 1994 House Elections in Perspective," *Political Science Quarterly* 111 (1996), 203–23. On the Contract with America: John Ferejohn, "A Tale of Two Congresses: Social Policy in the Clinton Years," in Margaret Weir (ed.), *The Social Divide: Political Parties and the Future of Activist Government* (Washington, D.C.: Brookings Institution, 1998).

This being the case, what do members actually do? "Loyalty is evidently calculated; the general rule seems to be that, when the pulls of party and constituency conflict, go with the party only if the expected electoral penalty will not significantly increase your chances of losing your seat."[7] To be sure, it is probably *not* in line with the argument of this book for members to stick *with* their party on voter-losing enterprises, as many of them often do. This behavior arguably amounts to "shirking" (although the intense preferences of a party's activist core back home ordinarily intrude into an argument like this one at this point). Yet, from the standpoint of parties as analytic units, the findings cited above point to a powerful engine of dissensus and defection. If centrist defecting can count, ruling congressional parties can get "rolled" by cross-party floor majorities when they are on the wrong side of public opinion. That often happens. A perfect example is the McCain-Feingold (or Shays-Meehan) campaign-finance reform, which cleared the Senate in early 2001 through a "roll" of the Republican party leadership, then cleared the House in early 2002 through a similar "roll." Or in pre-rolls, so to speak, measures may never reach the floor at all. In the most spectacular instance of recent times, Clinton's ambitious health-care measure of 1993–94 never came to any House vote. According to Speaker Tom Foley, notwithstanding a Democratic

7. Jacobson and Bovitz, "The Electoral Politics of Budgets and Deficits," p. 21.

membership edge in the eighties: "There wasn't anything out there they wanted to vote for. We weren't close to a [floor] majority on any specific health care plan."[8]

On another aspect of congressional behavior, there is a recent finding of relevance: To a significant degree, House members seem to be rewarded or punished *individually* by voters according to their levels of roll-call support for presidents. It's not just a party thing.[9] In general, the member-centered electoral drive seems to be alive and well on Capitol Hill.

8. Haynes Johnson and David S. Broder, *The System: The American Way of Politics at the Breaking Point* (Boston: Little, Brown, 1996), p. 509.

9. Paul Gronke, Jeffrey Koch, and J. Matthew Wilson, "Follow the Leader? Presidential Approval, Presidential Support, and Representatives' Electoral Fortunes," *Journal of Politics* 65 (2003), 785–808.

ACKNOWLEDGMENTS

For their most useful comments as I was preparing this work I should like to thank Chris Achen, Albert Cover, Joseph La Palombara, David Price, Douglas Rae, and David Seidman. All of the arguments in the following pages are mine except the ones I have explicitly appropriated from others.

INTRODUCTION

How to study legislative behavior is a question that does not yield a consensual answer among political scientists. An ethic of conceptual pluralism prevails in the field, and no doubt it should. If there is any consensus, it is on the point that scholarly treatments should offer explanations—that they should go beyond descriptive accounts of legislators and legislatures to supply general statements about why both of them do what they do. What constitutes a persuasive explanation? In their contemporary quest to find out, legislative students have ranged far and wide, sometimes borrowing or plundering explanatory styles from the neighboring social sciences.

The most important borrowing has been from sociology. In fact it is fair to say that legislative research in the 1950s and 1960s had a dominant sociological tone to it. The literature abounded in terms like *role, norm, system,* and *socialization.* We learned that some United States senators adopt an "outsider" role;[1] that the House Appropriations Committee can

1. Ralph K. Huitt, "The Outsider in the Senate: An Alternative Role," ch. 4 in Huitt and Robert L. Peabody (eds.), *Congress: Two Decades of Analysis* (New York: Harper and Row, 1969).

usefully be viewed as a self-maintaining system;[2] that legislators can be categorized as "trustees," "politicos," or "delegates";[3] that the United States Senate has "folkways." [4] These findings and others like them grew out of research based for the first time on systematic elite interviewing.

From no other social science has borrowing been so direct or so important. But it is possible to point to writings that have shared—or partly shared—a root assumption of economics. The difference between economic and sociological explanation is sharp. As Niskanen puts it, "the 'compositive' method of economics, which develops hypotheses about social behavior from models of purposive behavior by individuals, contrasts with the 'collectivist' method of sociology, which develops hypotheses about social behavior from models of role behavior by aggregative ideal types." [5] To my knowledge no political scientist has explicitly anchored his legislative research in economics, but a number have in one way or another invoked "purposive behavior" as a guide to explanation. Thus there

2. Richard F. Fenno, Jr., *The Power of the Purse* (Boston: Little, Brown and Co., 1966), ch. 5.

3. John C. Wahlke et al., *The Legislative System* (New York: Wiley, 1962), ch. 12; Roger H. Davidson, *The Role of the Congressman* (New York: Pegasus, 1969), ch. 4.

4. Donald R. Matthews, *U.S. Senators and Their World* (Chapel Hill: University of North Carolina Press, 1960), ch. 5.

5. William A. Niskanen, *Bureaucracy and Representative Government* (New York: Aldine-Atherton, 1971), p. 5.

are three articles by Scher in which he posits the conditions under which congressmen will find it in their interest to engage in legislative oversight.[6] Other examples are Wildavsky's work on bargaining in the budgetary process[7] and Riker's general work on coalition building with its legislative applications.[8] More recently Manley and Fenno have given a clear purposive thrust to their important committee studies.[9] Fenno's thinking has evolved to the point where he now places a strong emphasis on detecting why congressmen join specific committees and what they get out of being members of them.

There is probably a disciplinary drift toward the purposive, a drift, so to speak, from the sociological toward the economic. If so, it occurs at a time when

6. Seymour Scher, "Congressional Committee Members as Independent Agency Overseers: A Case Study," 54 *American Political Science Review* 911–20 (1960); "The Politics of Agency Organization," 15 *Western Political Quarterly* 328–44 (1962); "Conditions for Legislative Control," 25 *Journal of Politics* 526–51 (1963).

7. Aaron Wildavsky, *The Politics of the Budgetary Process* (Boston: Little, Brown and Co., 1964).

8. William H. Riker, *The Theory of Political Coalitions* (New Haven: Yale University Press, 1962), with ch. 7 specifically on Congress; also William H. Riker and Donald Niemi, "The Stability of Coalitions in the House of Representatives," 56 *American Political Science Review* 58–65 (1962).

9. John F. Manley, *The Politics of Finance: The House Committee on Ways and Means* (Boston: Little, Brown and Co., 1970); Richard F. Fenno, Jr., *Congressmen in Committees* (Boston: Little, Brown and Co., 1973).

some economists are themselves edging over into the legislative field. There is Lindblom's writing on the politics of partisan mutual adjustment, with its legislative ramifications.[10] More generally there are recent writings of economists in the public finance tradition.[11] Public finance has its normative and empirical sides, the former best exemplified here in the discussion of legislative decision making offered by Buchanan and Tullock.[12] Niskanen develops the empirical side in his work positing bureaus as budget maximizers—an effort that leads him to hypothesize about the relations between bureaus and legislative committees.[13] Public finance scholars seem to have become interested in legislative studies as a result of their abandoning the old idea of the Benthamite legislator; that is, they have come to display a concern for what public officials

10. Charles E. Lindblom, *The Intelligence of Democracy* (New York: Free Press, 1965).

11. A suitable characterization of this tradition: "The theory of public finance has addressed itself to the questions of how much money should be spent on public expenditures, how these expenditures should be distributed among different public wants, and how the costs should be distributed between present and future, and among the members of the society." James S. Coleman, "Individual Interests and Collective Action," in Gordon Tullock (ed.), *Papers on Non-Market Decision-Making* (Charlottesville: Thomas Jefferson Center for Political Economy, University of Virginia, 1966).

12. James M. Buchanan and Gordon Tullock, *The Calculus of Consent* (Ann Arbor: University of Michigan Press, 1967), part III.

13. Niskanen, *Bureaucracy and Representative Government.*

actually do rather than an assumption that officials will automatically translate good policy into law once somebody finds out what it is.[14] With political scientists exploring the purposive and economists the legislative, there are at least three forms that future relations between writers in the two disciplines could take. First, scholars in both could continue to disregard each other's writings. Second, they could engage in an unseemly struggle over turf. Third, they could use each other's insights to develop collectively a more vigorous legislative scholarship in the style of political economy.

All this is an introduction to a statement of what I intend to do in the following essay. Mostly through personal experience on Capitol Hill, I have become convinced that scrutiny of purposive behavior offers the best route to an understanding of legislatures—or at least of the United States Congress. In the fashion of economics, I shall make a simple abstract assumption about human motivation and then speculate about the consequences of behavior based on that motivation. Specifically, I shall conjure up a vision of United States congressmen as single-minded seekers of reelection, see what kinds of activity that goal implies, and

14. There is a discussion of this point in Nathan Rosenberg, "Efficiency in the Government Sector: Discussion," 54 *American Economic Review* 251–52 (May 1954); and in James M. Buchanan, *Public Finance in Democratic Process* (Chapel Hill: University of North Carolina Press, 1967), p. 173.

then speculate about how congressmen so motivated are likely to go about building and sustaining legislative institutions and making policy. At all points I shall try to match the abstract with the factual.

I find an emphasis on the reelection goal attractive for a number of reasons. First, I think it fits political reality rather well. Second, it puts the spotlight directly on men rather than on parties and pressure groups, which in the past have often entered discussions of American politics as analytic phantoms. Third, I think politics is best studied as a struggle among men to gain and maintain power and the consequences of that struggle. Fourth—and perhaps most important—the reelection quest establishes an accountability relationship with an electorate, and any serious thinking about democratic theory has to give a central place to the question of accountability. The abstract assumption notwithstanding, I regard this venture as an exercise in political science rather than economics. Leaving aside the fact that I have no economics expertise to display, I find that economists who study legislatures bring to bear interests different from those of political scientists. Not surprisingly the public finance scholars tend to look upon government as a device for spending money. I shall give some attention to spending, but also to other governmental activities such as the production of binding rules. And I shall touch upon such traditional subjects of political science as elections, parties, governmental structure, and regime stability. Another distinction here is that economics research tends to be infused with the normative assumption that policy decisions should be judged by how well they meet the standard of Pareto optimality. This is an assumption that I do not share and that I do not think most political scientists share. There will be no need here to set forth any alternative assumption. I may say, for the record, that I find the model of proper legislative activity offered by Rawls a good deal more edifying than any that could be built on a foundation of Pareto optimality.[15]

My subject of concern here is a single legislative institution, the United States Congress. In many ways, of course, the Congress is a unique or unusual body. It is probably the most highly "professionalized" of legislatures, in the sense that it promotes careerism among its members and gives them the salaries, staff, and other resources to sustain careers.[16] Its parties are exceptionally diffuse. It is widely thought to be especially "strong" among legislatures as a checker of executive power. Like most Latin American legislatures but unlike most European ones, it labors in the shadow of a separately elected executive. My decision

15. John Rawls, *A Theory of Justice* (Cambridge: Harvard University Press, 1971), chs. 4 and 5, and especially pp. 274–84.
16. The term is from H. Douglas Price, "Computer Simulation and Legislative 'Professionalism': Some Quantitative Approaches to Legislative Evolution," paper presented to the annual convention of the American Political Science Association, 1970.

to focus on the Congress flows from a belief that there is something to be gained in an intensive analysis of a particular and important institution. But there is something general to be gained as well, for the exceptionalist argument should not be carried too far. In a good many ways the Congress is just one in a large family of legislative bodies. I shall find it useful at various points in the analysis to invoke comparisons with European parliaments and with American state legislatures and city councils. I shall ponder the question of what "functions" the Congress performs or is capable of performing—a question that can be answered only with the records of other legislatures in mind. Functions to be given special attention are those of legislating, overseeing the executive, expressing public opinion, and servicing constituents. No functional capabilities can be automatically assumed.[17] Indeed the very term *legislature* is an unfortunate one because it confuses structure and function. Accordingly I shall here on use the more awkward but more neutral term *representative assembly* to refer to members of the class of entities inhabited by the United States House and Senate. Whatever the noun, the identifying

17. "But it is equally true, though only of late and slowly beginning to be acknowledged, that a numerous assembly is as little fitted for the direct business of legislation as for that of administration." John Stuart Mill, *Considerations on Representative Government* (Chicago: Regency, 1962), p. 104.

characteristics of institutions in the class have been well stated by Loewenberg: it is true of all such entities that (1) "their members are formally equal to each other in status, distinguishing parliaments from hierarchically ordered organizations," and (2) "the authority of their members depends on their claim to representing the rest of the community, in some sense of that protean concept, representation." [18]

The following discussion will take the form of an extended theoretical essay. Perforce it will raise more questions than it answers. As is the custom in monocausal ventures, it will no doubt carry arguments to the point of exaggeration; finally, of course, I shall be satisfied to explain a significant part of the variance rather than all of it. What the discussion will yield, I hope, is a picture of what the United States Congress looks like if the reelection quest is examined seriously. The essay will be heavily footnoted, with the references serving as a running bibliographical guide to works by political scientists, economists, journalists, and politicians I have found useful in thinking about the subject. Part 1 will deal with the electoral incentive and the activities it induces. Part 2 will deal with institutional arrangements in Congress and with congressional policy making.

18. Gerhard Loewenberg, "The Role of Parliaments in Modern Political Systems," in Loewenberg (ed.), *Modern Parliaments: Change or Decline?* (Chicago: Aldine-Atherton, 1971), p. 3.

1

THE ELECTORAL INCENTIVE

Congress has declined into a battle for individual survival. Each of the Congressmen and each of the Senators has the attitude: "I've got to look out for myself." If you remember the old best advice you ever had in the army, it wound up with: "Never volunteer." This applies to Congress, and so we have very few volunteers. Most of them are willing only to follow those things that will protect them and give them the coloration which allows them to blend into their respective districts or their respective states. If you don't stick your neck out, you don't get it chopped off.

—Senator William B. Saxbe (R., Ohio)

The discussion to come will hinge on the assumption that United States congressmen[1] are interested in getting reelected—indeed, in their role here as abstractions, interested in nothing else. Any such assumption necessarily does some violence to the facts, so it is important at the outset to root this one as firmly as possible in reality. A number of questions about that reality immediately arise.

First, is it true that the United States Congress is a place where members wish to stay once they get there? Clearly there are representative assemblies that do not hold their members for very long. Members of the Colombian parliament tend to serve single terms and then move on.[2] Voluntary turnover is quite high in some American state legislatures—for example, in Alabama. In his study of the unreformed Connecticut legislature, Barber labeled some of his subjects "reluctants"—people not very much interested in politics who were briefly pushed into it by others.[3] An ethic of

1. Where the context does not suggest otherwise, the term *congressmen* will refer to members of both House and Senate.
2. James L. Payne, *Patterns of Conflict in Colombia* (New Haven: Yale University Press, 1968), pp. 19–20.
3. James D. Barber, *The Lawmakers* (New Haven: Yale University Press, 1965), ch. 4.

"volunteerism" pervades the politics of California city councils.[4] And in the Congress itself voluntary turnover was high throughout most of the nineteenth century.

Yet in the modern Congress the "congressional career" is unmistakably upon us.[5] Turnover figures show that over the past century increasing proportions of members in any given Congress have been holdovers from previous Congresses—members who have both sought reelection and won it. Membership turnover noticeably declined among southern senators as early as the 1850s, among senators generally just after the Civil War.[6] The House followed close behind, with turnover dipping in the late nineteenth century and continuing to decline throughout the twentieth.[7] Average number of terms served has gone up and up, with the House in 1971 registering an all-time high of 20 percent of its members who had served at least ten terms.[8] It seems fair to characterize the modern

4. Kenneth Prewitt, "Political Ambitions, Volunteerism, and Electoral Accountability," 64 *American Political Science Review* 5–17 (1970).

5. H. Douglas Price, "The Congressional Career Then and Now," ch. 2 in Nelson W. Polsby (ed.), *Congressional Behavior* (New York: Random House, 1971).

6. Price, "Computer Simulation and Legislative 'Professionalism,'" pp. 14–16.

7. Nelson W. Polsby, "The Institutionalization of the U.S. House of Representatives," 62 *American Political Science Review* 146 (1968).

8. Charles S. Bullock III, "House Careerists: Changing Patterns

Congress as an assembly of professional politicians spinning out political careers. The jobs offer good pay and high prestige. There is no want of applicants for them. Successful pursuit of a career requires continual reelection.[9]

A second question is this: even if congressmen seek reelection, does it make sense to attribute that goal to them to the exclusion of all other goals? Of course the answer is that a complete explanation (if one were possible) of a congressman's or any one else's behavior would require attention to more than just one goal. There are even occasional congressmen who intentionally do things that make their own electoral survival difficult or impossible. The late President Kennedy wrote of congressional "profiles in courage." [10] Former Senator Paul Douglas (D., Ill.) tells of how he tried to persuade Senator Frank Graham (D., N.C.) to tailor his issue positions in order to survive a 1950 primary. Graham, a liberal appointee to the office, refused to listen. He was a "saint," says Douglas.[11] He lost his

---

of Longevity and Attrition," 66 *American Political Science Review* 1296 (1972).

9. Indeed, it has been proposed that professional politicians could be gotten rid of by making reelection impossible. For a plan to select one-term legislators by random sampling of the population, see Dennis C. Mueller et al., "Representative Government via Random Selection," 12 *Public Choice* 57–68 (1972).

10. John F. Kennedy, *Profiles in Courage* (New York: Harper and Row, 1956).

11. Paul H. Douglas, *In the Fullness of Time* (New York: Harcourt Brace Jovanovich, 1972), pp. 238–41.

primary. There are not many saints. But surely it is common for congressmen to seek other ends alongside the electoral one and not necessarily incompatible with it. Some try to get rich in office, a quest that may or may not interfere with reelection.[12] Fenno assigns three prime goals to congressmen—getting reelected but also achieving influence within Congress and making "good public policy."[13] These latter two will be given attention further on in this discussion. Anyone can point to contemporary congressmen whose public activities are not obviously reducible to the electoral explanation; Senator J. William Fulbright (D., Ark.) comes to mind. Yet, saints aside, the electoral goal has an attractive universality to it. It has to be the *proximate* goal of everyone, the goal that must be achieved over and over if other ends are to be entertained. One former congressman writes, "All members of Congress have a primary interest in getting re-elected. Some members have no other interest."[14] Reelection underlies everything else, as

12. In the case of the late Senator Thomas Dodd (D., Conn.) these two goals apparently conflicted. See James Boyd, *Above the Law* (New York: New American Library, 1968). Using office for financial profit is probably less common in Congress than in some of the state legislatures (e.g. Illinois and New Jersey).

13. Fenno, *Congressmen in Committees*, p. 1.

14. Frank E. Smith (D., Miss.), *Congressman from Mississippi* (New York: Random House, 1964), p. 127. It will not be necessary here to reach the question of whether it is possible to detect the goals of congressmen by asking them what they are, or indeed the

indeed it should if we are to expect that the relation between politicians and public will be one of accountability.[15] What justifies a focus on the reelection goal is the juxtaposition of these two aspects of it—its putative empirical primacy and its importance as an accountability link. For analytic purposes, therefore, congressmen will be treated in the pages to come as if they were single-minded reelection seekers. Whatever else they may seek will be given passing attention, but the analysis will center on the electoral connection.

Yet another question arises. Even if congressmen are single-mindedly interested in reelection, are they in a position as individuals to do anything about it? If they

question of whether there are unconscious motives lurking behind conscious ones. In Lasswell's formulation "political types" are power seekers, with "private motives displaced on public objects rationalized in terms of public interest." Harold D. Lasswell, *Power and Personality* (New York: Viking, 1948), p. 38.

15. Of other kinds of relations we are entitled to be suspicious. "There can be no doubt, that if power is granted to a body of men, called Representatives, they, like any other men, will use their power, not for the advantage of the community, but for their own advantage, if they can. The only question is, therefore, how can they be prevented?" James Mill, "Government," in *Essays on Government, Jurisprudence, Liberty of the Press, and Law of Nations* (New York: Augustus M. Kelley, 1967), p. 18. Madison's view was that the United States House, by design the popular branch, "should have an immediate dependence on, and an intimate sympathy with, the people. Frequent elections are unquestionably the only policy by which this dependency and sympathy can be effectively secured." *The Federalist Papers*, selected and edited by Roy Fairfield (Garden City, N.Y.: Doubleday Anchor, 1961), no. 52, p. 165.

are not, if they are inexorably shoved to and fro by forces in their political environments, then obviously it makes no sense to pay much attention to their individual activities. This question requires a complex answer, and it will be useful to begin reaching for one by pondering whether individual congressmen are the proper analytic units in an investigation of this sort. An important alternative view is that parties rather than lone politicians are the prime movers in electoral politics. The now classic account of what a competitive political universe will look like with parties as its analytic units is Downs's *Economic Theory of Democracy*.[16] In the familiar Downsian world parties are entirely selfish. They seek the rewards of office, but in order to achieve them they have to win office and keep it. They bid for favor before the public as highly cohesive point-source "teams." A party enjoys complete control over government during its term in office and uses its control solely to try to win the next election. In a two-party system a voter decides how to cast his ballot by examining the record and promises of the party in power and the previous record and current promises of the party out of power; he then calculates an "expected party differential" for the coming term, con-

16. Anthony Downs, *An Economic Theory of Democracy* (New York: Harper and Row, 1957). Downs gives a formal touch to a political science literature of both normative and empirical importance, extending from Woodrow Wilson through E. E. Schattschneider and V. O. Key, Jr.

sults his own policy preferences, and votes accordingly. These are the essential lineaments of the theory.[17] Legislative representatives appear only as modest "intermediaries." If of the governing party they gather information on grassroots preferences and relay it to the government, and they try to persuade constituents back home that the government is doing a worthy job.[18]

How well a party model of this kind captures the reality of any given regime is an empirical question. One difficulty lies in the need for parties as cohesive teams (members whose "goals can be viewed as a simple, consistent preference-ordering").[19] In all non-autocratic regimes governments are made up of a plurality of elective officials—not just one man. How can a group of men be bound together so that it looks something like a Downsian team? Probably nowhere (in a nonautocratic regime) does a group achieve the ultimate fusion of preference-orderings needed to satisfy the model; party government in Britain, for

17. Ibid., chs. 2, 3.

18. Ibid., pp. 88–90. Because the information and opinions supplied by representatives are important in decision making, Downs says that in effect some decision power devolves to the representatives. But there is this constraint: "Theoretically, the government will continue to decentralize its power until the marginal gain in votes from greater conformity to popular desires is outweighed by the marginal cost in votes of lesser ability to co-ordinate its actions." Pp. 89–90.

19. Ibid., p. 26.

example, proceeds substantially by intraparty bargaining.[20] Nonetheless, it is plain that some regimes fit the model better than others. For some purposes it is quite useful to study British politics by using parties as analytic units. Britain, to start with, has a constitution that readily permits majoritarian government. But, beyond that, at the roll call stage British M.P.'s act as cohesive party blocs that look something like teams. It is not inevitable that they should do so, and indeed there was a good deal of individualistic voting in the Commons in the mid-nineteenth century.[21] Why do contemporary M.P.'s submit to party discipline? There are at least three reasons why they do so, and it will be profitable here to examine them in order to allow later contrasts with the American regime.

First of all, in both British parties the nominating systems are geared to produce candidates who will vote the party line if and when they reach Parliament. This happens not because nominations are centrally controlled, but because the local nominating outfits are small elite groups that serve in effect as nationally oriented cheerleaders for the Commons party leadership.[22]

20. See, for example, Richard E. Neustadt, "White House and Whitehall," *The Public Interest*, Winter 1966, pp. 55–69.

21. See William O. Aydelotte, "Voting Patterns in the British House of Commons in the 1840's," 5 *Comparative Studies in Society and History*, 134–63 (1963).

22. Austin Ranney, *Pathways to Parliament: Candidate Selection in Britain* (Madison: University of Wisconsin Press, 1965), p. 281;

Second, British M.P.'s lack the resources to set up shop as politicians with bases independent of party. Television time in campaigns goes to parties rather than to scattered independent politicians.[23] By custom or rule or both, the two parties sharply limit the funds that parliamentary candidates can spend on their own in campaigns.[24] Once elected, M.P.'s are not supplied the kinds of office resources—staff help, free mailing privileges, and the like—that can be used to achieve public salience.[25] These arguments should not be carried too far; M.P.'s are not ciphers, and obviously dissident leaders like Aneurin Bevan and Enoch Powell manage to build important independent fol-

---

Leon D. Epstein, "British M.P.'s and Their Local Parties: The Suez Case," 54 *American Political Science Review* 385–86 (1960).

23. Jay G. Blumler and Denis McQuail, *Television in Politics* (Chicago: University of Chicago Press, 1969), pp. xi–xxviii.

24. R. T. McKenzie, *British Political Parties* (New York: St. Martin's, 1955), pp. 252–53, 555.

25. "An American Congressman, it is said, collapsed with shock on being shown the writing-rooms and the Library of the Commons full of men writing letters in longhand: members of Parliament answering the constituency mail." Bernard Crick, *The Reform of Parliament* (Garden City, N.Y.: Doubleday, 1965), p. 58; and, generally, Crick, pp. 58–59. Things have changed somewhat since Crick's account, but the contrast is still valid. See also Anthony Barker and Michael Rush, *The Member of Parliament and His Information* (London: Allen and Unwin, 1970). Loewenberg reports that, in West Germany, "the average member of the Bundestag works under Spartan conditions." Gerhard Loewenberg, *Parliament in the German Political System* (Ithaca: Cornell University Press, 1967), p. 53.

lowings. But the average backbencher is constrained by lack of resources. It comes as no surprise that individual M.P.'s add little to (or subtract little from) core partisan electoral strength in their constituencies; the lion's share of the variance in vote change from election to election is chargeable to national swings rather than to local or regional fluctuations.[26]

Third, with the executive entrenched in Parliament the only posts worth holding in a Commons career are the ones doled out by party leaders. Up to a third of majority party M.P.'s are now included in the Ministry.[27] "For the ambitious backbencher, the task is to impress ministers and particularly the Prime Minister." [28] Party loyalty is rewarded; heresy is not.

The upshot of all this is that British M.P.'s are locked in. The arrangement of incentives and resources elevates parties over politicians. But the United States is very different. In America the underpinnings of "teamsmanship" are weak or absent, making it possible for politicians to triumph over

26. Donald E. Stokes, "Parties and the Nationalization of Electoral Forces," ch. 7 in William N. Chambers and Walter D. Burnham, *The American Party Systems* (New York: Oxford University Press, 1967), pp. 188–89.

27. Crick, *The Reform of Parliament*, pp. 30–31. Crick adds: "A modern Prime Minister has a patronage beyond the wildest dreams of political avarice of a Walpole or a Newcastle." P. 31.

28. John P. Mackintosh, "Reform of the House of Commons: The Case for Specialization," in Loewenberg (ed.), *Modern Parliaments*, p. 39.

parties. It should be said that Madisonian structure and Downsian teamsmanship are not necessarily incompatible.[29] Connecticut state government, in which party organizations exercise substantial control over nominations and political careers, comes close to the British model; governorship and state legislative parties are bound together by party organization.[30] But Connecticut is exceptional, or, more accurately, it is at one end of a spectrum toward the other end of which there are states in which parties have little binding effect at all.[31] In American politics the place

29. Indeed in city studies there is the standard functional case that cohesive parties may arise to deal with problems caused by constitutional diffusion. See, for example, on Chicago, Edward C. Banfield, *Political Influence* (New York: Free Press, 1961), ch. 8. American parties have traditionally been strongest at the municipal level. But something interesting happens to Downs on the way to the city. Where parties are held together by patronage, and where there are no geographically subsidiary governments that can serve as independent political bases, there is a strong tendency for party politics to become monopolistic rather than competitive. Ambitious politicians have little incentive to sustain an opposition party and every incentive to join the ruling party. The same argument generally holds for national politics in mid-eighteenth-century England.

30. See Duane Lockard, *New England State Politics* (Princeton: Princeton University Press, 1965), chs. 9, 10; Joseph I. Lieberman, *The Power Broker* (Boston: Houghton Mifflin, 1966); James D. Barber, "Leadership Strategies for Legislative Party Cohesion," 28 *Journal of Politics* 347–67 (1966).

31. In the California Senate, for example, at least until recently, committee chairmanships were given out to the most senior

where Downsian logic really applies is in the election
of individuals to executive posts—presidents, governors, and big city mayors. To choose among candidates for the presidency or the New York City
mayoralty is to choose among "executive teams"—
candidates with their retinues of future high administrators, financial supporters, ghost-writers, pollsters,
student ideologues, journalistic flacks, hangers-on, occasionally burglars and spies. In executive elections
the candidates are highly visible; they bid for favor in
Downsian fashion; they substantially control government (or appear to) and can be charged with its
accomplishments and derelictions (President Nixon for
inflation, Mayor Lindsay for crime); elections are
typically close (now even in most old machine cities);
voters can traffic in "expected differentials" (between
executive candidates rather than parties). When the
late V. O. Key, Jr., wrote *The Responsible Electorate*,[32] a
book in the Downsian spirit, he had the empirical
good sense to focus on competition between incumbent
and prospective presidential administrations rather
than more broadly on competition between parties.
Indeed, it can be argued that American representative
assemblies have declined in power in the twentieth

members regardless of party. Alvin D. Sokolow and Richard W.
Brandsma, "Partisanship and Seniority in Legislative Committee
Assignments: California after Reapportionment," 24 *Western Politi-
cal Quarterly* 741–47 (1971).

32. Cambridge: Harvard University Press, 1966.

century (especially at the city council level) and executives have risen chiefly because it is the executives who offer electorates something like Downsian accountability.[33]

But at the congressional level the teamsmanship model breaks down. To hark back to the discussion of Britain, the specified resource and incentive arrangements conducive to party unity among M.P.'s are absent in the congressional environment: First, the way in which congressional candidates win party nominations is not, to say the least, one that fosters party cohesion in Congress. For one thing, 435 House members and 98 senators (all but the Indiana pair) are now nominated by direct primary (or can be, in the few states with challenge primaries) rather than by caucus or convention. There is no reason to expect large primary electorates to honor party loyalty. (An introduction of the direct primary system in Britain might in itself destroy party cohesion in the Commons.) For another, even where party organizations are still strong enough to control congressional primaries,[34] the parties are locally rather than

33. There is Huntington's point that sweeping turnover of a Jacksonian sort now occurs in national politics only at the top executive level. Samuel P. Huntington, "Congressional Responses to the Twentieth Century," ch. 1 in David B. Truman (ed.), *The Congress and America's Future* (Englewood Cliffs, N.J.: Prentice-Hall, 1965), p. 17.

34. In Chicago, for example. See Leo M. Snowiss, "Congres-

nationally oriented; local party unity is vital to them, national party unity is not. Apparently it never has been.[35]

Second, unlike the M.P. the typical American congressman has to mobilize his own resources initially to win a nomination and then to win election and reelection. He builds his own electoral coalition and sustains it. He raises and spends a great deal of money in doing so. He has at his command an elaborate set of electoral resources that the Congress bestows upon all its members. There will be more on these points later. The important point here is that a congressman can—indeed must—build a power base that is substantially independent of party.[36] In the words of a House member quoted by Clapp, "If we depended on

sional Recruitment and Representation," 60 *American Political Science Review* 627–39 (1966).

35. On the fluid behavior of machine congressmen back when there were a good many more of them, see Moisei Ostrogorski, *Democracy and the Organization of Political Parties*, vol. II, *The United States* (Garden City, N.Y.: Doubleday, 1964), pp. 286–89. Tammany Democrats broke party ranks to save Speaker Joseph G. Cannon from Insurgent and Democratic attack in the Sixtieth Congress, a year before his downfall. See Blair Bolles, *Tyrant from Illinois* (New York: Norton, 1951), p. 181.

36. See Charles L. Clapp, *The Congressman: His Work as He Sees It* (Washington, D.C.: Brookings, 1963), pp. 30–31; Robert J. Huckshorn and Robert C. Spencer, *The Politics of Defeat* (Amherst, Mass.: University of Massachusetts Press, 1971), pp. vii, 71–72; David A. Leuthold, *Electioneering in a Democracy* (New York: Wiley, 1968), passim.

the party organization to get elected, none of us would be here." [37]

Third, Congress does not have to sustain a cabinet and hence does not engage the ambitions of its members in cabinet formation in such a fashion as to induce party cohesion. It would be wrong to posit a general one-to-one relation here between party cohesion and cabinet sustenance. On the one hand, there is nothing preventing congressmen from building disciplined congressional parties anyway if they wanted to do so. On the other hand, as the records of the Third and Fourth French republics show, cabinet regimes can be anchored in relatively incohesive parties. Yet, to pose the proposition in statistical rather than deterministic form, the need for an assembly to sustain a cabinet probably raises the likelihood that it will spawn disciplined parties.[38]

The fact is that no theoretical treatment of the United States Congress that posits parties as analytic units will go very far. So we are left with individual congressmen, with 535 men and women rather than two parties, as units to be examined in the discussion to come. The style of argument will be somewhat like that of Downs, but the reality more like that of Namier.[39] Whether the choice of units is propitious

37. Clapp, *The Congressman*, p. 351.

38. See the argument in Leon D. Epstein, "A Comparative Study of Canadian Parties," 58 *American Political Science Review* 46–59 (1964).

39. Lewis Namier, *The Structure of Politics at the Accession of George*

can be shown only in the facts marshaled and the arguments embellished around them. With the units nailed down, still left unanswered is the question of whether congressmen in search of reelection are in a position to do anything about it.

Here it will be useful to deal first with the minority subset of congressmen who serve marginal districts or states—constituencies fairly evenly balanced between the parties. The reason for taking up the marginals separately is to consider whether their electoral precariousness ought to induce them to engage in distinctive electoral activities. Marginals have an obvious problem; to a substantial degree they are at the mercy of national partisan electoral swings. But general voter awareness of congressional legislative activities is low.[40] Hence national swings in the congressional vote are normally judgments on what the president is doing (or is thought to be doing) rather than on what Congress is doing. In the familiar case where parties controlling the presidency lose House seats in the midterm, swings seem to be not judgments on anything at all but rather artifacts of the election cycle.[41] More along a judgmen-

III (London: Macmillan, 1960). For a Namier passage on assemblies without disciplined parties see p. 17.

40. Donald E. Stokes and Warren E. Miller, "Party Government and the Saliency of Congress," ch. 11 in Angus Campbell et al., *Elections and the Political Order* (New York: Wiley, 1966), p. 199.

41. Angus Campbell, "Surge and Decline: A Study of Electoral Change," ch. 3 in ibid.; Barbara Hinckley, "Interpreting House

tal line, there has been an impressive relation over the years between partisan voting for the House and ups and downs in real income among voters. The national electorate rewards the congressional party of a president who reigns during economic prosperity and punishes the party of one who reigns during adversity.[42] Rewards and penalties may be given by the same circuitous route for other states of affairs, including national involvement in wars.[43] With voters behaving the way they do, it is in the electoral interest of a marginal congressman to help insure that a presidential administration of his own party is a popular success or that one of the opposite party is a failure. (Purely from the standpoint of electoral interest there is no reason why a congressman with a safe seat should care one way or another.)

But what can a marginal congressman do to affect the fortunes of a presidency? One shorthand course a marginal serving under a president of his own party can take is to support him diligently in roll call voting; there is ambiguous evidence that relevant marginals

Midterm Elections: Toward a Measurement of the In-Party's 'Expected' Loss of Seats," 61 *American Political Science Review* 694–700 (1967).

42. Gerald H. Kramer, "Short-Term Fluctuations in U.S. Voting Behavior, 1896–1964," 65 *American Political Science Review* 131–43 (1971). See also the symposium on the Kramer findings in 63 *American Economic Review* 160–80 (May 1973).

43. Kramer, "U.S. Voting Behavior," p. 140. Wars seem to earn penalties.

do behave disproportionately in this fashion.[44] This
strategy may not always be the best one. During the
1958 recession, for example, it may have been wise for
marginal Republicans to support Democratic deficit-
spending bills over the opposition of President Eisenhower; in the 1958 election Eisenhower's policies seem
to have been ruinous for members of his own party.
How about marginals of the opposition party? By the
same logic it might be advantageous for opposition
marginals to try to wreck the economy; if it were done
unobtrusively the voters would probably blame the
president, not them.

There are a number of intriguing theoretical possibilities here for marginals of parties both in and out of
power. Yet marginals seem not to pay much attention
to strategies of this sort, whether ingenuous or ingenious. What we are pondering is whether individual
marginals can realistically hope to do anything to
affect the national component of the variance over
time in congressional partisan election percentages.[45]
And the answer seems to be no—or at least extraordinarily little. Leaving aside the problem of generating
collective congressional action, there is the root problem of knowing what to try to do. It is hard to point to
an instance in recent decades in which any group of

44. David B. Truman, *The Congressional Party* (New York: Wiley,
1959), pp. 213–18.
45. As in Stokes, "Parties and the Nationalization of Electoral
Forces."

congressmen (marginals or not) has done something that has clearly changed the national congressional electoral percentage in a direction in which the group intended to change it (or to keep it stationary if that was the intention). There are too many imponderables. Most importantly, presidents follow their own logic. So do events. Not even economists can have a clear idea about what the effects of economic measures will be. The election cycle adds its own kind of perversity; the vigorous enactment of President Johnson's Great Society legislation (by all the survey evidence popular) was followed in 1966 by the largest Republican gain in House popular vote percentage of the last quarter century. Hence there is a lack of usable lore among congressmen on what legislative actions will produce what national electoral effects.[46]

46. Nonetheless there are interesting questions here that have never been explored. Do marginal congressmen—or members generally—of the party not in control of the presidency try to sabotage the economy? Of course they must not appear to do so, but there are "respectable" ways of acting. How about Republicans in the Eightieth Congress with their tax cutting in time of inflation? Or Democrats with their spending programs under President Nixon—also in a time of inflation? The answer is probably no. It would have to be shown that the same congressmen's actions differ under presidencies of different parties, and they probably do not. Strategies like this not only require duplicity, they require a vigorous consciousness of distant effects of a sort that is foreign to the congressional mentality.

And there is after all the problem of generating collective action—especially action among nonmarginal congressmen who can watch national election percentages oscillate and presidents come and go with relative equanimity. All in all the rational way for marginal congressmen to deal with national trends is to ignore them, to treat them as acts of God over which they can exercise no control. It makes much more sense to devote resources to things over which they think they can have some control. There is evidence that marginals do think and act distinctively. House marginals are more likely than nonmarginals to turn up as "district-oriented" and "delegates" in role studies;[47] they introduce more floor amendments;[48] in general marginals of both houses display more frenzy in their election-oriented activities. But these activities are not directed toward affecting national election percentages. And although they may differ in intensity, they do not differ in kind from the activities engaged in by everybody else.

Are, then, congressmen in a position to do anything about getting reelected? If an answer is sought in their ability to affect national partisan percentages, the answer is no. But if an answer is sought in their ability to affect the percentages in their own primary and

47. Davidson, *Role of the Congressman*, p. 128.
48. David M. Olson and Cynthia T. Nonidez, "Measures of Legislative Performance in the U.S. House of Representatives," 16 *Midwest Journal of Political Science* 273–74 (1972).

general elections, the answer is yes. Or at least so the case will be presented here. More specifically, it will be argued that they think that they can affect their own percentages, that in fact they can affect their own percentages, and furthermore that there is reason for them to try to do so. This last is obvious for the marginals, but perhaps not so obvious for the nonmarginals. Are they not, after all, occupants of "safe seats"? It is easy to form an image of congressmen who inherit lush party pastures and then graze their way through careers without ever having to worry about elections. But this image is misconceived, and it is important to show why.

First, when looked at from the standpoint of a career, congressional seats are not as safe as they may seem. Of House members serving in the Ninety-third Congress 58 percent had at least one time in their careers won general elections with less than 55 percent of the total vote, 77 percent with less than 60 percent of the vote. For senators the figures were 70 percent and 86 percent (the last figure including fifteen of the twenty-two southerners). And aside from these November results there is competition in the primaries. The fact is that the typical congressman at least occasionally has won a narrow victory.[49]

49. Over the long haul the proportion of seats switching from party to party is quite surprising. Of senators serving in the Ninety-third Congress, 56 had succeeded members of the opposite party in initially coming to the Senate, 43 had succeeded members

Second—to look at the election figures from a different angle—in United States House elections only about a third of the variance in partisan percentages over time is attributable to national swings. About half the variance is local (or, more properly, residual, the variance not explained by national and state components).[50] The local component is probably at least as high in Senate elections. Hence vote variation over which congressmen have reason to think they can exercise some control (i.e. the primary vote and the local component of the November vote) is substantial. What this comes down to in general elections is that district vote fluctuations beyond or in opposition to national trends can be quite striking. For example,

of the same party, and 1 (Hiram Fong: R., Hawaii) had come into the Senate at the same time his state entered the union. (Predecessors here are taken to be the last elected predecessors; i.e. interim appointees are ignored.) Of House members serving in the same Congress, 157 had originally succeeded members of the opposite party; 223 members of the same party; and 55 had originally taken newly created seats. (District continuity at the time of member transition is assumed here if a new district took in substantially the same territory as an old one.)

50. Stokes, "Parties and the Nationalization of Electoral Forces," p. 186. Thus the American ranking of vote components in order of importance differs from the British ranking. Richard S. Katz has recently introduced a measurement technique that yields higher national components. Katz, "The Attribution of Variance in Electoral Returns: An Alternative Measurement Technique," 67 *American Political Science Review* 817–28 (1973). But the British-American disparity presumably remains. There is a Stokes rejoinder at pp. 829–34.

between 1968 and 1970 the Republican share of the national House vote fell 3.3 percent, but the share of Congressman Chester L. Mize (R., Kans.) fell from 67.6 percent to 45.0 percent, and he lost his seat. In 1972 four incumbent Republican senators lost their seats; in general 1972 was not a bad year for congressional Republicans, and all four senators had won in 1966 with at least 58 percent of the vote. And so it goes. In addition, there are the primaries.[51] It is hard for anyone to feel absolutely secure in an electoral environment of this sort. In Kingdon's interview study of candidates who had just run for office in Wisconsin (about a third of them running for Congress) the proportion who recalled having been "uncertain" about electoral outcome during their campaigns was high, and the incidence of uncertainty was only modestly related to actual electoral outcome.[52]

51. In the 1964-72 period ten House committee chairmen lost their primaries.

52. John W. Kingdon, *Candidates for Office: Beliefs and Strategies* (New York: Random House, 1968), pp. 86–89. Richard F. Fenno, Jr., who has recently been traveling with incumbent congressmen in their districts—some of them very "safe" districts indeed—detects a pervasive feeling of electoral insecurity: "One of the dominant impressions of my travels is the terrific sense of *uncertainty* which animates these congressmen. They perceive electoral troubles where the most imaginative outside observer could not possibly perceive, conjure up or hallucinate them." Fenno, "Congressmen in Their Constituencies," unpublished manuscript, pp. 6–7.

But the local vote component cuts two ways; if losses are possible, so presumably are gains. In particular, it seems to be possible for some incumbents to beef up their November percentages beyond normal party levels in their constituencies. In the House (but apparently not in the Senate) the overall electoral value of incumbency seems to have risen in the last decade[53]—although of course some House incumbents still do lose their seats.

Third, there is a more basic point. The ultimate

53. From about 2 percent in the 1950s to about 5 percent in 1966 and maybe higher in 1970–72. See Robert S. Erikson, "The Advantage of Incumbency in Congressional Elections," 3 *Polity* 395–405 (1971); Erikson, "Malapportionment, Gerrymandering, and Party Fortunes in Congressional Elections," 66 *American Political Science Review* 1240 (1972); David R. Mayhew, "Congressional Elections: The Case of the Vanishing Marginals," forthcoming in *Polity*, Spring 1974. It is not clear what accounts for the rise in incumbency value, not even certain that it is attributable to the election-oriented activities of incumbents. But some of the electoral sagas of recent years are truly startling. There is the case of the Wisconsin seventh district, strongly Republican for years in the hands of Melvin R. Laird. Laird's last percentages were 65.1 percent in 1966 and 64.1 percent in 1968. When Laird went to the cabinet, David R. Obey took the seat for the Democrats with 51.6 percent in a 1969 by-election. Obey won with 67.6 percent in 1970 and then with 63.5 percent in a 1972 election in which he was forced to run against an incumbent Republican in a merged district. On Obey's election-oriented activities see Norman C. Miller, "Privileges of Rank: New Congressman Finds Campaigning Is Easier Now That He's in Office," *Wall Street Journal*, August 4, 1969, p. 1.

concern here is not how probable it is that legislators will lose their seats but whether there is a connection between what they do in office and their need to be reelected. It is possible to conceive of an assembly in which no member ever comes close to losing a seat but in which the need to be reelected is what inspires members' behavior. It would be an assembly with no saints or fools in it, an assembly packed with skilled politicians going about their business. When we say "Congressman Smith is unbeatable," we do not mean that there is nothing he could do that would lose him his seat. Rather we mean, "Congressman Smith is unbeatable as long as he continues to do the things he is doing." If he stopped answering his mail, or stopped visiting his district, or began voting randomly on roll calls, or shifted his vote record eighty points on the ADA scale, he would bring on primary or November election troubles in a hurry. It is difficult to offer conclusive proof that this last statement is true, for there is no congressman willing to make the experiment. But normal political activity among politicians with healthy electoral margins should not be confused with inactivity. What characterizes "safe" congressmen is not that they are beyond electoral reach, but that their efforts are very likely to bring them uninterrupted electoral success.

Whether congressmen think their activities have electoral impact, and whether in fact they have impact, are of course two separate questions. Of the former there can be little doubt that the answer is yes. In fact in their own minds successful politicians probably overestimate the impact they are having. Kingdon found in his Wisconsin candidates a "congratulation-rationalization effect," a tendency for winners to take personal credit for their victories and for losers to assign their losses to forces beyond their control.[54] The actual impact of politicians' activities is more difficult to assess. The evidence on the point is soft and scattered. It is hard to find variance in activities undertaken, for there are no politicians who consciously try to lose. There is no doubt that the electorate's general awareness of what is going on in Congress is something less than robust.[55] Yet the argument here will be that congressmen's activities in fact do have electoral impact. Pieces of evidence will be brought in as the discussion proceeds.[56]

54. Kingdon, *Candidates for Office*, p. 31. Charles S. Bullock III has recently found the same effect in a study of United States House incumbents and challengers in the 1972 election. Bullock, "Candidate Perceptions of Causes of Election Outcome," paper presented to the annual convention of the American Political Science Association, 1973.

55. Stokes and Miller, "Party Government."

56. The most sophisticated treatment of this subject is in Warren E. Miller and Donald E. Stokes, "Constituency Influence in Congress," ch. 16 in Campbell et al., *Elections and the Political Order*, pp. 366–70. Note that a weird but important kind of accountability relationship would exist if congressmen thought their activities had impact even if in fact they had none at all.

The next step here is to offer a brief conceptual treatment of the relation between congressmen and their electorates. In the Downsian analysis what national party leaders must worry about is voters' "expected party differential." [57] But to congressmen this is in practice irrelevant, for reasons specified earlier. A congressman's attention must rather be devoted to what can be called an "expected incumbent differential." Let us define this "expected incumbent differential" as any difference perceived by a relevant political actor between what an incumbent congressman is likely to do if returned to office and what any possible challenger (in primary or general election) would be likely to do. And let us define "relevant political actor" here as anyone who has a resource that might be used in the election in question. At the ballot box the only usable resources are votes, but there are resources that can be translated into votes: money, the ability to make persuasive endorsements, organizational skills, and so on. By this definition a "relevant political actor" need not be a constituent; one of the most important resources, money, flows all over the country in congressional campaign years.[58]

57. Downs, *Economic Theory of Democracy*, pp. 38–45.
58. To give an extreme example, in the North Dakota Senate campaign of 1970 an estimated 85 to 90 percent of the money spent by candidates of both parties came from out of state. Philip M. Stern, *The Rape of the Taxpayer* (New York: Random House, 1973), p. 384.

It must be emphasized that the average voter has only the haziest awareness of what an incumbent congressman is actually doing in office.[59] But an incumbent has to be concerned about actors who do form impressions about him, and especially about actors who can marshal resources other than their own votes. Senator Robert C. Byrd (D., W.Va.) has a "little list" of 2,545 West Virginians he regularly keeps in touch with.[60] A congressman's assistant interviewed for a Nader profile in 1972 refers to the "thought leadership" back in the district.[61] Of campaign re-

59. For thousands of November voters totally unaware of candidate particularities, the commonest election criterion is no doubt the party label on the ballot. These voters are normally left undisturbed in their ignorance, although candidates may find it useful to deploy resources to get the right ones to the polls. But it must not be assumed that there are no circumstances under which such voters can be aroused into vigorous candidate awareness.

60. Robert Sherrill, "The Embodiment of Poor White Power," *New York Times Magazine*, February 28, 1971, p. 51.

61. Ellen Szita, Ralph Nader Congress Project profile on Garner E. Shriver (R., Kans.) (Washington, D.C.: Grossman, 1972), p. 14. Shriver's administrative assistant was asked about the district value of the congressman's Appropriations Committee membership. His answer: "Projectwise, it's been valuable. . . . I wouldn't say the majority of his constituents recognize that the Appropriations Committee is one of the most important—just those I would term the 'thought leadership' in the district." The interviewer adds that it must be the "community leadership in Wichita" the assistant was referring to, for, when asked, "with few exceptions . . . the leaders listed more than ten different federally-subsidized projects that Representative Shriver had brought to the

sources one of the most vital is money. An incumbent not only has to assure that his own election funds are adequate, he has to try to minimize the probability that actors will bankroll an expensive campaign against him. There is the story that during the first Nixon term Senator James B. Pearson (R., Kans.) was told he would face a well-financed opponent in his 1972 primary if he did not display more party regularity in his voting.[62] Availability of money can affect strength of opposition candidacy in both primary and general elections.[63]

---

fourth district." (Congress Project profiles referred to in future footnotes will be called "Nader profiles" for short. For all of them the more complete citation is the one given here.)

62. Dennis Harvey, "How GOP Sen. Pearson Went from Sure Loser to Sure Winner in 1972," *Wall Street Journal*, September 29, 1972, p. 1.

63. There is the following report of an election problem suffered by Congressman Torbert H. Macdonald (D., Mass.), chairman of the Communications and Power Subcommittee of the House Interstate and Foreign Commerce Committee: "His fear of opposition from some of these industries is so overwhelming that they have succeeded in immobilizing him with regard to regulatory legislation. For example several years ago he received a political scare when the electric companies bankrolled his opponent in the general election. Since then, according to [Congressman Robert O.] Tiernan [D., R.I.], 'Macdonald will not touch them.' That interpretation is confirmed by Macdonald's former aid, Marty Kuhn, who states that 'Even though Torby easily defeated his opponent, the experience made him sort of paranoid. He is now reluctant to do anything that would offend the power people.' " John Paris's chapter on "Communications" in David E.

Another resource of significance is organizational expertise, probably more important than money among labor union offerings. Simple ability to do electioneering footwork is a resource the invoking of which may give campaigns an interesting twist. Leuthold found in studying ten 1962 House elections in the San Francisco area that 50 percent of campaign workers held college degrees (as against 12 percent of the Bay area population), and that the workers were more issue oriented than the general population.[64] The need to attract workers may induce candidates to traffic in issues more than they otherwise would. Former Congressman Allard K. Lowenstein (D., N.Y.) has as his key invokable resource a corps of student volunteers who will follow him from district to district, making him an unusually mobile candidate.

Still another highly important resource is the ability to make persuasive endorsements. Manhattan candidates angle for the imprimatur of the *New York Times.* New Hampshire politics rotates around endorsements of the *Manchester Union Leader.* Labor union committees circulate their approved lists. Chicago Democratic politicians seek the endorsement of the mayor. In the San Francisco area and elsewhere House candidates

Price (ed.), "The House and Senate Committees on Commerce" (unpublished manuscript), p. 161. The reference is apparently to the election of 1968, when Macdonald's percentage fell to 62.5. It is normally well over 65.

64. Leuthold, *Electioneering in a Democracy*, pp. 92–94.

try to score points by winning endorsements from officials of the opposite party.[65] As Neustadt argues, the influence of the president over congressmen (of both parties) varies with his public prestige and with his perceived ability to punish and reward.[66] One presidential tool is the endorsement, which can be carefully calibrated according to level of fervor, and which can be given to congressmen or to challengers running against congressmen. In the 1970 election Senator Charles Goodell (R., N.Y.), who had achieved public salience by attacking the Nixon administration, was apparently done in by the resources called forth by that attack; the vice president implicitly endorsed his Conservative opponent, and the administration acted to channel normally Republican money away from Goodell.[67]

What a congressman has to try to do is to insure that in primary and general elections the resource balance (with all other deployed resources finally translated into votes) favors himself rather than somebody else. To maneuver successfully he must remain

65. Ibid., p. 44.

66. Richard E. Neustadt, *Presidential Power* (New York: New American Library, 1964), chs. 4, 5.

67. Of course when the president's poll ratings drop, so do his ability to punish and reward and his influence over congressmen. When they drop very low, it becomes politically profitable for congressmen of his own party to attack him—as with Democrats in 1951–52 and Republicans in 1973–74.

constantly aware of what political actors' incumbent differential readings are, and he must act in a fashion to inspire readings that favor himself. Complicating his task is the problem of slack resources. That is, only a very small proportion of the resources (other than votes) that are conceivably deployable in congressional campaigns are ever in fact deployed. But there is no sure way of telling who will suddenly become aroused and with what consequence. For example, just after the 1948 election the American Medical Association, unnerved by the medical program of the Attlee Government in Britain and by Democratic campaign promises here to institute national health insurance, decided to venture into politics. By 1950 congressmen on record as supporters of health insurance found themselves confronted by a million-dollar AMA advertising drive, local "healing arts committees" making candidate endorsements, and even doctors sending out campaign literature with their monthly bills. By 1952 it was widely believed that the AMA had decided some elections, and few congressmen were still mentioning health insurance.[68]

In all his calculations the congressman must keep in

68. "The American Medical Association: Power, Purpose, and Politics in Organized Medicine," 63 *Yale Law Journal* 1011–18 (1954). Senator Douglas's recollection: "Legislators accepted the conclusion that the voters were opposed to all forms of health insurance and that they should avoid an open conflict with the AMA." Douglas, *In the Fullness of Time*, p. 390.

mind that he is serving two electorates rather than one—a November electorate and a primary electorate nested inside it but not a representative sample of it. From the standpoint of the politician a primary is just another election to be survived.[69] A typical scientific poll of a constituency yields a congressman information on the public standing of possible challengers in the other party but also in his own party. A threat is a threat. For an incumbent with a firm "supporting coalition"[70] of elite groups in his party the primary electorate is normally quiescent. But there can be sudden turbulence. And it sometimes happens that the median views of primary and November electorates are so divergent on salient issues that a congressman finds it difficult to hold both electorates at once. This has been a recurrent problem among California Republicans.[71]

69. The convention system of the late nineteenth century offered comparable perils. Bryce comments that House seats were highly prized and that there was an ethic that they should be rotated. "An ambitious Congressman is therefore forced to think day and night of his re-nomination, and to secure it not only by procuring, if he can, grants from the Federal Treasury for local purposes, and places for the relatives and friends of the local wire-pullers who control the nominating conventions, but also by sedulously 'nursing' the constituency during the vacations." James Bryce, *The American Commonwealth* (New York: Putnam's, 1959), I: 40–41.

70. The term is Kingdon's. *Candidates for Office*, p. 45.

71. Although the direct primary system is uniquely American, there are variants that pose similar problems for politicians. In

A final conceptual point has to do with whether congressmen's behavior should be characterized as "maximizing" behavior. Does it make sense to visualize the congressman as a maximizer of vote percentage in elections—November or primary or, with some complex trade-off, both? For two reasons the answer is probably no. The first has to do with his goal itself, which is to stay in office rather than to win all the popular vote. More precisely his goal is to stay in office over a number of future elections, which does mean that "winning comfortably" in any one of them (except the last) is more desirable than winning by a narrow plurality. The logic here is that a narrow victory (in primary or general election) is a sign of weakness that can inspire hostile political actors to deploy resources intensively the next time around. By this reasoning the higher the election percentages the better. No doubt any congressman would engage in an act to raise his November figure from 80 percent to 90

Italian parliamentary elections each voter registers a vote for a favored party's candidate list, but then can also cast preference votes for individual candidates on that list. Whether a given candidate gets elected depends both on how well his party does against other parties and how well he does against nominees of his own party. Mass organizations (e.g. labor and farm groups) capable of mobilizing preference votes reap benefits in the parliament, "where nothing seems to count so much as the ability to deliver the required number of preference votes." Joseph LaPalombara, *Interest Groups in Italian Politics* (Princeton: Princeton University Press, 1964), pp. 248–49.

percent if he could be absolutely sure that the act would accomplish the end (without affecting his primary percentage) and if it could be undertaken at low personal cost. But still, trying to "win comfortably" is not the same as trying to win all the popular vote. As the personal cost (e.g. expenditure of personal energy) of a hypothetical "sure gain" rises, the congressman at the 55 percent November level is more likely to be willing to pay it than his colleague at the 80 percent level.

The second and more decisive reason why a pure maximization model is inappropriate is that congressmen act in an environment of high uncertainty. An assumption of minimax behavior therefore gives a better fit. Behavior of an innovative sort can yield vote gains, but it can also bring disaster (as in Senator Goodell's case). For the most part it makes sense for congressmen to follow conservative strategies. Each member, after all, is a recent victor of two elections (primary and general), and it is only reasonable for him to believe that whatever it was that won for him the last time is good enough to win the next time. When a congressman has a contented primary electorate and a comfortable November percentage, it makes sense to sit tight, to try to keep the coalition together. Where November constituencies are polarized in the conventional fashion—labor and liberals on one side, business on the other—there is hardly any alternative. Yet simply repeating the activities of the past is of course impossible, for the world changes. There are always new voters, new events, new issues. Congressmen therefore need conservative strategies for dealing with change. And they have some. For members with conventional supporting coalitions it can be useful to accept party cues in deciding how to cast roll call votes;[72] a Republican House member from Indiana can hardly go wrong in following the party line (though for an Alabama Democrat or a Massachusetts Republican it would be madness to do so). It may be useful to build a voting record that blends in with the records of party colleagues in one's state delegation.[73] It is surely useful to watch other members' primary and general elections to try to gain clues on voter temperament. But conservatism can be carried only so

72. On cues generally see Donald R. Matthews and James A. Stimson, "Cue-Taking by Congressmen: A Model and a Computer Simulation," paper presented at Conference on the Use of Quantitative Methods in the Study of the History of Legislative Behavior, 1972; and John E. Jackson, "Statistical Models of Senate Roll Call Voting," 65 *American Political Science Review* 451–70 (1971).

73. See Aage Clausen, *How Congressmen Decide: A Policy Focus* (New York: St. Martin's Press, 1973), ch. 7. Fiellin writes on the New York delegation: "Most important of all, perhaps, is that the member in taking cues from the New York group cannot get into electoral difficulties as a result of deviation. There is security in numbers." Alan Fiellin, "The Functions of Informal Groups: A State Delegation," ch. 3 in Robert L. Peabody and Nelson W. Polsby (eds.), *New Perspectives on the House of Representatives* (Chicago: Rand McNally, 1969), p. 113.

far. It requires a modest degree of venturesomeness just to hold an old coalition together. And for members in great electoral danger (again, Goodell) it may on balance be wise to resort to ostentatious innovation.

Whether they are safe or marginal, cautious or audacious, congressmen must constantly engage in activities related to reelection. There will be differences in emphasis, but all members share the root need to do things—indeed, to do things day in and day out during their terms. The next step here is to present a typology, a short list of the *kinds* of activities congressmen find it electorally useful to engage in. The case will be that there are three basic kinds of activities. It will be important to lay them out with some care, for arguments in part 2 will be built on them.

One activity is *advertising,* defined here as any effort to disseminate one's name among constituents in such a fashion as to create a favorable image but in messages having little or no issue content. A successful congressman builds what amounts to a brand name, which may have a generalized electoral value for other politicians in the same family. The personal qualities to emphasize are experience, knowledge, responsiveness, concern, sincerity, independence, and the like. Just getting one's name across is difficult enough; only about half the electorate, if asked, can supply their House members' names. It helps a congressman to be known. "In the main, recognition carries a positive valence; to be perceived at all is to be perceived favorably." [74] A vital advantage enjoyed by House incumbents is that they are much better known among voters than their November challengers.[75] They are better known because they spend a great deal of time, energy, and money trying to make themselves better known.[76] There are standard routines—frequent visits to the constituency, nonpolitical speeches to home audiences,[77] the sending out of infant care booklets and letters of condolence and congratulation. Of 158 House members questioned in the mid-1960s, 121 said that they regularly sent newsletters to their constituents;[78] 48 wrote separate news or opinion columns for newspapers; 82 regularly reported to their constituen-

74. Stokes and Miller, "Party Government," p. 205. The same may not be true among, say, mayors.

75. Ibid., p. 204. The likelihood is that senators are also better known than their challengers, but that the gap is not so wide as it is on the House side. There is no hard evidence on the point.

76. In Clapp's interview study, "Conversations with more than fifty House members uncovered only one who seemed to place little emphasis on strategies designed to increase communications with the voter." *The Congressman*, p. 88. The exception was an innocent freshman.

77. A statement by one of Clapp's congressmen: "The best speech is a non-political speech. I think a commencement speech is the best of all. X says he has never lost a precinct in a town where he has made a commencement speech." *The Congressman*, p. 96.

78. These and the following figures on member activity are from Donald G. Tacheron and Morris K. Udall, *The Job of the Congressman* (Indianapolis: Bobbs-Merrill, 1966), pp. 281–88.

cies by radio or television;[79] 89 regularly sent out mail questionnaires.[80] Some routines are less standard. Congressman George E. Shipley (D., Ill.) claims to have met personally about half his constituents (i.e. some 200,000 people).[81] For over twenty years Congressman Charles C. Diggs, Jr. (D., Mich.) has run a radio program featuring himself as a "combination disc jockey–commentator and minister." [82] Congressman Daniel J. Flood (D., Pa.) is "famous for appearing unannounced and often uninvited at wedding anniversaries and other events." [83] Anniversaries and other events aside, congressional advertising is done

79. Another Clapp congressman: "I was looking at my TV film today—I have done one every week since I have been here—and who was behind me but Congressman X. I'll swear he had never done a TV show before in his life but he only won by a few hundred votes last time. Now he has a weekly television show. If he had done that before he wouldn't have had any trouble." *The Congressman*, p. 92.

80. On questionnaires generally see Walter Wilcox, "The Congressional Poll—and Non-Poll," in Edward C. Dreyer and Walter A. Rosenbaum (eds.), *Political Opinion and Electoral Behavior* (Belmont, Calif.: Wadsworth, 1966), pp. 390–400.

81. Szita, Nader profile on Shipley, p. 12. The congressman is also a certified diver. "When Shipley is home in his district and a drowning occurs, he is sometimes asked to dive down for the body. 'It gets in the papers and actually, it's pretty good publicity for me,' he admitted." P. 3. Whether this should be classified under "casework" rather than "advertising" is difficult to say.

82. Lenore Cooley, Nader profile on Diggs, p. 2.

83. Anne Zandman and Arthur Magida, Nader profile on Flood, p. 2.

largely at public expense. Use of the franking privilege has mushroomed in recent years; in early 1973 one estimate predicted that House and Senate members would send out about 476 million pieces of mail in the year 1974, at a public cost of $38.1 million—or about 900,000 pieces per member with a subsidy of $70,000 per member.[84] By far the heaviest mailroom traffic comes in Octobers of even-numbered years.[85] There are some differences between House and Senate members in the ways they go about getting their names across. House members are free to blanket their constituencies with mailings for all boxholders; senators are not. But senators find it easier to appear on national television—for example, in short reaction statements on the nightly news shows. Advertising is a staple congressional activity, and there is no end to it. For each member there are always new voters to be apprised of his worthiness and old voters to be reminded of it.[86]

A second activity may be called *credit claiming,* defined here as acting so as to generate a belief in a

84. Norman C. Miller, "Yes, You Are Getting More Politico Mail: And It Will Get Worse," *Wall Street Journal,* March 6, 1973, p. 1.

85. Monthly data compiled by Albert Cover.

86. After serving his two terms, the late President Eisenhower had this conclusion: "There is nothing a Congressman likes better than to get his name in the headlines and for it to be published all over the United States." From a 1961 speech quoted in the *New York Times,* June 20, 1971.

relevant political actor (or actors) that one is personally responsible for causing the government, or some
unit thereof, to do something that the actor (or actors)
considers desirable. The political logic of this, from the
congressman's point of view, is that an actor who
believes that a member can make pleasing things
happen will no doubt wish to keep him in office so that
he can make pleasing things happen in the future. The
emphasis here is on individual accomplishment (rather
than, say, party or governmental accomplishment)
and on the congressman as doer (rather than as, say,
expounder of constituency views). Credit claiming is
highly important to congressmen, with the consequence that much of congressional life is a relentless
search for opportunities to engage in it.

Where can credit be found? If there were only one
congressman rather than 535, the answer would in
principle be simple enough.[87] Credit (or blame) would
attach in Downsian fashion to the doings of the
government as a whole. But there are 535. Hence it
becomes necessary for each congressman to try to peel
off pieces of governmental accomplishment for which
he can believably generate a sense of responsibility.
For the average congressman the staple way of doing
this is to traffic in what may be called "particularized
benefits."[88] Particularized governmental benefits, as

87. In practice the one might call out the army and suspend the
Constitution.
88. These have some of the properties of what Lowi calls

the term will be used here, have two properties: (1) Each benefit is given out to a specific individual, group, or geographical constituency, the recipient unit being of a scale that allows a single congressman to be recognized (by relevant political actors and other congressmen) as the claimant for the benefit (other congressmen being perceived as indifferent or hostile). (2) Each benefit is given out in apparently ad hoc fashion (unlike, say, social security checks) with a congressman apparently having a hand in the allocation. A particularized benefit can normally be regarded as a member of a class. That is, a benefit given out to an individual, group, or constituency can normally be looked upon by congressmen as one of a class of similar benefits given out to sizable numbers of individuals, groups, or constituencies. Hence the impression can arise that a congressman is getting "his share" of whatever it is the government is offering. (The classes may be vaguely defined. Some state legislatures deal in what their members call "local legislation.")

In sheer volume the bulk of particularized benefits come under the heading of "casework"—the thousands of favors congressional offices perform for supplicants in ways that normally do not require legislative

---

"distributive" benefits. Theodore J. Lowi, "American Business, Public Policy, Case-Studies, and Political Theory," 16 *World Politics* 690 (1964).

action. High school students ask for essay materials, soldiers for emergency leaves, pensioners for location of missing checks, local governments for grant information, and on and on. Each office has skilled professionals who can play the bureaucracy like an organ— pushing the right pedals to produce the desired effects.[89] But many benefits require new legislation, or at least they require important allocative decisions on matters covered by existent legislation. Here the congressman fills the traditional role of supplier of goods to the home district. It is a believable role; when a member claims credit for a benefit on the order of a dam, he may well receive it.[90] Shiny construction projects seem especially useful.[91] In the decades before

89. On casework generally see Kenneth G. Olson, "The Service Function of the United States Congress," pp. 337–74 in American Enterprise Institute, *Congress: The First Branch of Government* (Washington, D.C.: American Enterprise Institute for Public Policy Research, 1966).

90. Sometimes without justification. Thus this comment by a Republican member of the House Public Works Committee: "The announcements for projects are an important part of this. . . . And the folks back home are funny about this—if your name is associated with it, you get all the credit whether you got it through or not." James T. Murphy, "Partisanship and the House Public Works Committee," paper presented to the annual convention of the American Political Science Association, 1968, p. 10.

91. "They've got to *see* something; it's the bread and butter issues that count—the dams, the post offices and the other public buildings, the highways. They want to know what you've been doing." A comment by a Democratic member of the House Public Works Committee. Ibid.

1934, tariff duties for local industries were a major commodity.[92] In recent years awards given under grant-in-aid programs have become more useful as they have become more numerous. Some quests for credit are ingenious; in 1971 the story broke that congressmen had been earmarking foreign aid money for specific projects in Israel in order to win favor with home constituents.[93] It should be said of constituency benefits that congressmen are quite capable of taking the initiative in drumming them up; that is, there can be no automatic assumption that a congressman's activity is the result of pressures brought to bear by organized interests. Fenno shows the importance of member initiative in his discussion of the House Interior Committee.[94]

A final point here has to do with geography. The examples given so far are all of benefits conferred upon home constituencies or recipients therein (the latter including the home residents who applauded the Israeli projects). But the properties of particularized benefits were carefully specified so as not to exclude

92. The classic account is in E. E. Schattschneider, *Politics, Pressures, and the Tariff* (New York: Prentice-Hall, 1935).

93. "Israeli Schools and Hospitals Seek Funds in Foreign-Aid Bill," *New York Times*, October 4, 1971, p. 10.

94. Fenno, *Congressmen in Committees*, p. 40. Cf. this statement on initiative in the French Third Republic: "Most deputies ardently championed the cause of interest groups in their district without waiting to be asked." Bernard E. Brown, "Pressure Politics in France," 18 *Journal of Politics* 718 (1956).

the possibility that some benefits may be given to recipients outside the home constituencies. Some probably are. Narrowly drawn tax loopholes qualify as particularized benefits, and some of them are probably conferred upon recipients outside the home districts.[95] (It is difficult to find solid evidence on the point.) Campaign contributions flow into districts from the outside, so it would not be surprising to find that benefits go where the resources are.[96]

How much particularized benefits count for at the polls is extraordinarily difficult to say. But it would be hard to find a congressman who thinks he can afford to wait around until precise information is available. The lore is that they count—furthermore, given home expectations, that they must be supplied in regular quantities for a member to stay electorally even with the board. Awareness of favors may spread beyond their recipients,[97] building for a member a general

95. For a discussion of the politics of tax loopholes see Stanley S. Surrey, "The Congress and the Tax Lobbyist—How Special Tax Provisions Get Enacted," 70 *Harvard Law Review* 1145–82 (1957).

96. A possible example of a transaction of this sort: During passage of the 1966 "Christmas tree" tax bill, Senator Vance Hartke (D., Ind.) won inclusion of an amendment giving a tax credit to a California aluminum firm with a plant in the Virgin Islands. George Lardner, Jr., "The Day Congress Played Santa," *Washington Post*, December 10, 1966, p. 10. Whether Hartke was getting campaign funds from the firm is not wholly clear, but Lardner's account allows the inference that he was.

97. Thus this comment of a Senate aide, "The world's greatest publicity organ is still the human mouth. . . . When you get

reputation as a good provider. "Rivers Delivers." "He Can Do More For Massachusetts." [98] A good example of Capitol Hill lore on electoral impact is given in this account of the activities of Congressman Frank Thompson, Jr. (D., N.J., 4th district):

> In 1966, the 4th was altered drastically by redistricting; it lost Burlington County and gained Hunterdon, Warren, and Sussex. Thompson's performance at the polls since 1966 is a case study of how an incumbent congressman, out of line with his district's ideological persuasions, can become unbeatable. In 1966, Thompson carried Mercer by 23,000 votes and lost the three new counties by 4,600, winning reelection with 56% of the votes. He then survived a district-wide drop in his vote two years later. In 1970, the Congressman carried Mercer County by 20,000 votes and the rest of the district by 6,000, finishing with 58%. The drop in Mercer

somebody $25.00 from the Social Security Administration, he talks to his friends and neighbors about it. After a while the story grows until you've single-handedly obtained $2,500 for a constituent who was on the brink of starvation." Matthews, *U.S. Senators*, p. 226.

98. For some examples of particularistically oriented congressmen see the Nader profiles by Sven Holmes on James A. Haley (D., Fla.), Newton Koltz on Joseph P. Addabbo (D., N.Y.), Alex Berlow on Kenneth J. Gray (D., Ill.), and Sarah Glazer on John Young (D., Tex.). For a fascinating picture of the things House members were expected to do half a century ago see Joe Martin, *My First Fifty Years in Politics* (New York: McGraw-Hill, 1960), pp. 55–59.

resulted from the attempt of his hard-line conservative opponent to exploit the racial unrest which had developed in Trenton. But for four years Thompson had been making friends in Hunterdon, Warren, and Sussex, busy doing the kind of chores that congressmen do. In this case, Thompson concerned himself with the interests of dairy farmers at the Department of Agriculture. The results of his efforts were clear when the results came in from the 4th's northern counties.[99]

So much for particularized benefits. But is credit available elsewhere? For governmental accomplishments beyond the scale of those already discussed? The general answer is that the prime mover role is a hard one to play on larger matters—at least before broad electorates. A claim, after all, has to be credible. If a congressman goes before an audience and says, "I am responsible for passing a bill to curb inflation," or "I am responsible for the highway program," hardly anyone will believe him. There are two reasons why people may be skeptical of such claims. First, there is a numbers problem. On an accomplishment of a sort that probably engaged the supportive interest of more than one member it is reasonable to suppose that credit should be apportioned among them. But second, there is an overwhelming problem of information costs.

99. Michael Barone, Grant Ujifusa, and Douglas Matthews, *The Almanac of American Politics* (Boston: Gambit, 1972), pp. 479–80.

For typical voters Capitol Hill is a distant and mysterious place; few have anything like a working knowledge of its maneuverings. Hence there is no easy way of knowing whether a congressman is staking a valid claim or not. The odds are that the information problem cuts in different ways on different kinds of issues. On particularized benefits it may work in a congressman's favor; he may get credit for the dam he had nothing to do with building. Sprinkling a district with dams, after all, is something a congressman is supposed to be able to do. But on larger matters it may work against him. For a voter lacking an easy way to sort out valid from invalid claims the sensible recourse is skepticism. Hence it is unlikely that congressmen get much mileage out of credit claiming on larger matters before broad electorates.[100]

Yet there is an obvious and important qualification here. For many congressmen credit claiming on non-particularized matters is possible in specialized subject areas because of the congressional division of labor. The term "governmental unit" in the original definition of credit claiming is broad enough to include committees, subcommittees, and the two houses of Congress itself. Thus many congressmen can believably claim credit for blocking bills in subcommittee,

committee work

100. Any teacher of American politics has had students ask about senators running for the presidency (Goldwater, McGovern, McCarthy, any of the Kennedys), "But what bills has he passed?" There is no unembarrassing answer.

adding on amendments in committee, and so on. The audience for transactions of this sort is usually small. But it may include important political actors (e.g. an interest group, the president, the *New York Times*, Ralph Nader) who are capable of both paying Capitol Hill information costs and deploying electoral resources. There is a well-documented example of this in Fenno's treatment of post office politics in the 1960s. The postal employee unions used to watch very closely the activities of the House and Senate Post Office Committees and supply valuable electoral resources (money, volunteer work) to members who did their bidding on salary bills.[101] Of course there are many examples of this kind of undertaking, and there is more to be said about it. The subject will be covered more exhaustively in part 2.

The third activity congressmen engage in may be called *position taking*, defined here as the public enunciation of a judgmental statement on anything likely to be of interest to political actors. The statement may take the form of a roll call vote. The most important classes of judgmental statements are those prescribing American governmental ends (a vote cast against the war; a statement that "the war should be ended immediately") or governmental means (a statement that "the way to end the war is to take it to the United Nations"). The judgments may be implicit rather than

101. Fenno, *Congressmen in Committees*, pp. 242–55.

explicit, as in: "I will support the president on this matter." But judgments may range far beyond these classes to take in implicit or explicit statements on what almost anybody should do or how he should do it: "The great Polish scientist Copernicus has been unjustly neglected"; "The way for Israel to achieve peace is to give up the Sinai." [102] The congressman as position taker is a speaker rather than a doer. The electoral requirement is not that he make pleasing things happen but that he make pleasing judgmental statements. The position itself is the political commodity. Especially on matters where governmental responsibility is widely diffused it is not surprising that political actors should fall back on positions as tests of incumbent virtue. For voters ignorant of congressional processes the recourse is an easy one. The following comment by one of Clapp's House interviewees is highly revealing: "Recently, I went home and began to talk about the ———— act. I was pleased to have sponsored that bill, but it soon dawned on me that the point wasn't getting through at all. What was getting through was that the act might be a help to people. I changed the emphasis: I didn't mention my role particularly, but stressed my support of the legislation." [103]

102. In the terminology of Stokes, statements may be on either "position issues" or "valence issues." Donald E. Stokes, "Spatial Models of Party Competition," ch. 9 in Campbell et al., *Elections and the Political Order*, pp. 170–74.

103. Clapp, *The Congressman*, p. 108. A difficult borderline question here is whether introduction of bills in Congress should be

The ways in which positions can be registered are numerous and often imaginative. There are floor addresses ranging from weighty orations to mass-produced "nationality day statements." [104] There are speeches before home groups, television appearances, letters, newsletters, press releases, ghostwritten books, *Playboy* articles, even interviews with political scientists. On occasion congressmen generate what amount to petitions; whether or not to sign the 1956 Southern Manifesto defying school desegregation rulings was an important decision for southern members.[105] Outside

---

counted under position taking or credit claiming. On balance probably under the former. Yet another Clapp congressman addresses the point: "I introduce about sixty bills a year, about 120 a Congress. I try to introduce bills that illustrate, by and large, my ideas—legislative, economic, and social. I do like being able to say when I get cornered, 'yes, boys, I introduced a bill to try to do that in 1954.' To me it is the perfect answer." Ibid., p. 141. But voters probably give claims like this about the value they deserve.

104. On floor speeches generally see Matthews, *U.S. Senators*, p. 247. On statements celebrating holidays cherished by ethnic groups, Hearings on the Organization of Congress before the Joint Committee on the Organization of the Congress, 89th Cong., 1st sess., 1965, p. 1127; and Arlen J. Large, "And Now Let's Toast Nicolaus Copernicus, the Famous German," *Wall Street Journal*, March 12, 1973, p. 1.

105. Sometimes members of the Senate ostentatiously line up as "cosponsors" of measures—an activity that may attract more attention than roll call voting itself. Thus in early 1973, seventy-six senators backed a provision to block trade concessions to the U.S.S.R. until the Soviet government allowed Jews to emigrate without paying high exit fees. " 'Why did so many people sign the

the roll call process the congressman is usually able to tailor his positions to suit his audiences. A solid consensus in the constituency calls for ringing declarations; for years the late Senator James K. Vardaman (D., Miss.) campaigned on a proposal to repeal the Fifteenth Amendment.[106] Division or uncertainty in the constituency calls for waffling; in the late 1960s a congressman had to be a poor politician indeed not to be able to come up with an inoffensive statement on Vietnam ("We must have peace with honor at the earliest possible moment consistent with the national interest"). On a controversial issue a Capitol Hill office normally prepares two form letters to send out to constituent letter writers—one for the pros and one (not directly contradictory) for the antis.[107] Handling discrete audiences in person requires simple agility, a talent well demonstrated in this selection from a Nader profile:

> "You may find this difficult to understand," said Democrat Edward R. Roybal, the Mexican-Ameri-

---

amendment?' a Northern Senator asked rhetorically. 'Because there is no political advantage in not signing. If you do sign, you don't offend anyone. If you don't sign, you might offend some Jews in your state.' " David E. Rosenbaum, "Firm Congress Stand on Jews in Soviet Is Traced to Efforts by Those in U.S.," *New York Times*, April 6, 1973, p. 14.

106. ". . . an utterly hopeless proposal and for that reason an ideal campaign issue." V. O. Key, Jr., *Southern Politics* (New York: Knopf, 1949), p. 232.

107. Instructions on how to do this are given in Tacheron and Udall, *Job of the Congressman*, pp. 73–74.

can representative from California's thirtieth district, "but sometimes I wind up making a patriotic speech one afternoon and later on that same day an anti-war speech. In the patriotic speech I speak of past wars but I also speak of the need to prevent more wars. My positions are not inconsistent; I just approach different people differently." Roybal went on to depict the diversity of crowds he speaks to: one afternoon he is surrounded by balding men wearing Veterans' caps and holding American flags; a few hours later he speaks to a crowd of Chicano youths, angry over American involvement in Vietnam. Such a diverse constituency, Roybal believes, calls for different methods of expressing one's convictions.[108]

Indeed it does. Versatility of this sort is occasionally possible in roll call voting. For example a congressman may vote one way on recommittal and the other on final passage, leaving it unclear just how he stands on a bill.[109] Members who cast identical votes on a measure may give different reasons for having done so. Yet it is on roll calls that the crunch comes; there is no way for a member to avoid making a record on

108. William Lazarus, Nader profile on Edward R. Roybal (D., Cal.), p. 1.

109. On obfuscation in congressional position taking see Raymond A. Bauer, Ithiel de Sola Pool, and Lewis A. Dexter, *American Business and Public Policy* (New York: Atherton, 1964), pp. 431–32.

Suggests these effects may unintentionally be misleading →

hundreds of issues, some of which are controversial in the home constituencies. Of course, most roll call positions considered in isolation are not likely to cause much of a ripple at home. But broad voting patterns can and do; member "ratings" calculated by the Americans for Democratic Action, Americans for Constitutional Action, and other outfits are used as guidelines in the deploying of electoral resources. And particular issues often have their alert publics. Some national interest groups watch the votes of all congressmen on single issues and ostentatiously try to reward or punish members for their positions; over the years some notable examples of such interest groups have been the Anti-Saloon League,[110] the early Farm Bureau,[111] the American Legion,[112] the American Medical Association,[113] and the National Rifle Associ-

110. "Elaborate indexes of politicians and their records were kept at Washington and in most of the states, and professions of sympathy were matched with deeds. The voters were constantly apprised of the doings of their representatives." Peter H. Odegard, *Pressure Politics: The Story of the Anti-Saloon League* (New York: Columbia University Press, 1928), p. 21.

111. On Farm Bureau dealings with congressmen in the 1920s see Orville M. Kile, *The Farm Bureau through Three Decades* (Baltimore: Waverly Press, 1948), ch. 7.

112. V. O. Key, Jr., "The Veterans and the House of Representatives: A Study of a Pressure Group and Electoral Mortality," 5 *Journal of Politics* 27–40 (1943).

113. "The American Medical Association," pp. 1011–18. See also Richard Harris, *A Sacred Trust* (New York: New American Library, 1966).

ation.[114] On rare occasions single roll calls achieve a rather high salience among the public generally. This seems especially true of the Senate, which every now and then winds up for what might be called a "showdown vote," with pressures on all sides, presidential involvement, media attention given to individual senators' positions, and suspense about the outcome. Examples are the votes on the nuclear test-ban treaty in 1963, civil rights cloture in 1964, civil rights cloture again in 1965, the Haynsworth appointment in 1969, the Carswell appointment in 1970, and the ABM in 1970. Controversies on roll calls like these are often relived in subsequent campaigns, the southern Senate elections of 1970 with their Haynsworth and Carswell issues being cases in point.

Probably the best position-taking strategy for most congressmen at most times is to be conservative—to cling to their own positions of the past where possible and to reach for new ones with great caution where necessary. Yet in an earlier discussion of strategy the suggestion was made that it might be rational for

114. On the NRA generally see Stanford N. Sesser, "The Gun: Kingpin of 'Gun Lobby' Has a Million Members, Much Clout in Congress," *Wall Street Journal*, May 24, 1972, p. 1. On the defeat of Senator Joseph Tydings (D., Md.) in 1970: "Tydings himself tended to blame the gun lobby, which in turn was quite willing to take the credit. 'Nobody in his right mind is going to take on that issue again [i.e. gun control],' one Tydings strategist admitted." John F. Bibby and Roger H. Davidson, *On Capitol Hill: Studies in the Legislative Process* (Hinsdale, Ill.: Dryden, 1972), p. 50.

members in electoral danger to resort to innovation. The form of innovation available is entrepreneurial position taking, its logic being that for a member facing defeat with his old array of positions it makes good sense to gamble on some new ones. It may be that congressional marginals fulfill an important function here as issue pioneers—experimenters who test out new issues and thereby show other politicians which ones are usable.[115] An example of such a pioneer is Senator Warren Magnuson (D., Wash.), who responded to a surprisingly narrow victory in 1962 by reaching for a reputation in the area of consumer affairs.[116] Another example is Senator Ernest Hollings (D., S.C.), a servant of a shaky and racially heterogeneous southern constituency who launched "hunger" as an issue in 1969—at once pointing to a problem and giving it a useful nonracial definition.[117] One of the

115. A cautious politician will not be sure of an issue until it has been tested in a campaign. Polling evidence is suggestive, but it can never be conclusive.

116. David Price, *Who Makes the Laws?* (Cambridge, Mass.: Schenkman, 1972), p. 29. Magnuson was chairman of the Senate Commerce Committee. "Onto the old Magnuson, interested in fishing, shipping, and Boeing Aircraft, and running a rather sleepy committee, was grafted a new one: the champion of the consumer, the national legislative leader, and the patron of an energetic and innovative legislative staff." P. 78.

117. Marjorie Hunter, "Hollings Fight on Hunger Is Stirring the South," *New York Times*, March 8, 1969, p. 14. The local reaction was favorable. "Already Senator Herman E. Talmadge, Democrat of Georgia, has indicated he will begin a hunger crusade

most successful issue entrepreneurs of recent decades was the late Senator Joseph McCarthy (R., Wis.); it was all there—the close primary in 1946, the fear of defeat in 1952, the desperate casting about for an issue, the famous 1950 dinner at the Colony Restaurant where suggestions were tendered, the decision that "Communism" might just do the trick.[118]

The effect of position taking on electoral behavior is about as hard to measure as the effect of credit claiming. Once again there is a variance problem; congressmen do not differ very much among themselves in the methods they use or the skills they display in attuning themselves to their diverse constituencies. All of them, after all, are professional politicians. There is intriguing hard evidence on some matters where variance can be captured. Schoenberger has found that House Republicans who signed an early pro-Goldwater petition plummeted significantly farther in their 1964 percentages than their colleagues who did not sign.[119] (The signers appeared genuinely

in his own state. Other Senators have hinted that they may do the same."

118. Robert Griffith, *The Politics of Fear: Joseph R. McCarthy and the Senate* (New York: Hayden, 1970), p. 29. Rovere's conclusion: "McCarthy took up the Communist menace in 1950 not with any expectation that it would make him a sovereign of the assemblies, but with the single hope that it would help him hold his job in 1952." Richard Rovere, *Senator Joe McCarthy* (Cleveland: World, 1961), p. 120.

119. Robert A. Schoenberger, "Campaign Strategy and Party Loyalty: The Electoral Relevance of Candidate Decision-Making

to believe that identification with Goldwater was an electoral plus.) Erikson has found that roll call records are interestingly related to election percentages: "[A] reasonable estimate is that an unusually liberal Republican Representative gets at least 6 per cent more of the two-party vote . . . than his extreme conservative counterpart would in the same district." [120] In other words, taking some roll call positions that please voters of the opposite party can be electorally helpful. (More specifically, it can help in November; some primary electorates will be more tolerant of it than others.) Sometimes an inspection of deviant cases offers clues. There is the ideological odyssey of former Congressman Walter Baring (D., Nev.), who entered Congress as a more or less regular Democrat in the mid-1950s but who moved over to a point where he was the most conservative House Democrat outside the South by the late 1960s. The Nevada electorate reacted predictably; Baring's November percentages rose astoundingly high (82.5 percent in 1970), but he encountered guerrilla warfare in the primaries which finally cost him his nomination in 1972—whereupon the seat turned Republican.

There can be no doubt that congressmen believe positions make a difference. An important conse-

---

in the 1964 Congressional Elections," 63 *American Political Science Review* 515–20 (1969).

120. Robert S. Erikson, "The Electoral Impact of Congressional Roll Call Voting," 65 *American Political Science Review* 1023 (1971).

quence of this belief is their custom of watching each other's elections to try to figure out what positions are salable. Nothing is more important in Capitol Hill politics than the shared conviction that election returns have proven a point. Thus the 1950 returns were read not only as a rejection of health insurance but as a ratification of McCarthyism.[121] When two North Carolina nonsigners of the 1956 Southern Manifesto immediately lost their primaries, the message was clear to southern members that there could be no straying from a hard line on the school desegregation issue. Any breath of life left in the cause of school bussing was squeezed out by House returns from the Detroit area in 1972. Senator Douglas gives an interesting report on the passage of the first minimum wage bill in the Seventy-fifth Congress. In 1937 the bill was tied up in the House Rules Committee, and there was an effort to get it to the floor through use of a discharge petition. Then two primary elections broke the jam. Claude Pepper (D., Fla.) and Lister Hill (D., Ala.) won nominations to fill vacant Senate seats. "Both campaigned on behalf of the Wages and Hours

121. Griffith, *The Politics of Fear*, pp. 122–31. The defeat of Senator Millard Tydings (D., Md.) was attributed to resources (money, endorsements, volunteer work) conferred or mobilized by McCarthy. "And if Tydings can be defeated, then who was safe? Even the most conservative and entrenched Democrats began to fear for their seats, and in the months that followed, the legend of McCarthy's political power grew." P. 123.

bill, and both won smashing victories. . . . Immediately after the results of the Florida and Alabama primaries became known, there was a stampede to sign the petition, and the necessary 218 signatures were quickly obtained." [122] The bill later passed. It may be useful to close this section on position taking with a piece of political lore on electoral impact that can stand beside the piece on the impact of credit claiming offered earlier. The discussion is of the pre-1972 sixth California House district:

> Since 1952 the district's congressman has been Republican William S. Mailliard, a wealthy member of an old California family. For many years Mailliard had a generally liberal voting record. He had no trouble at the polls, winning elections by large majorities in what is, by a small margin at least, a Democratic district. More recently, Mailliard seems caught between the increasing conservatism of the state's Republican party and the increasing liberalism of his constituency.
>
> After [Governor Ronald] Reagan's victory [in 1966], Mailliard's voting record became noticeably more conservative. Because of this, he has been spared the tough conservative primary opposition that Paul McCloskey has confronted in the 11th. But Mailliard's move to the right has not gone

122. Douglas, *In the Fullness of Time*, p. 140.

unnoticed in the 6th district. In 1968 he received 73% of the vote, but in 1970 he won only 53%—a highly unusual drop for an incumbent of such long standing. Much of the difference must be attributed to the war issue. San Francisco and Marin are both antiwar strongholds; but Mailliard, who is the ranking Republican on the House Foreign Affairs Committee, has supported the Nixon Administration's war policy. In the 6th district, at least, that position is a sure vote-loser.[123]

These, then, are the three kinds of electorally oriented activities congressmen engage in—advertising, credit claiming, and position taking. It remains only to offer some brief comments on the emphases different members give to the different activities. No deterministic statements can be made; within limits each member has freedom to build his own electoral coalition and hence freedom to choose the means of doing it.[124] Yet there are broad patterns. For one thing senators, with their access to the media, seem to put more emphasis on position taking than House members; probably House members rely more heavily on particularized benefits. But there are important differences among House members. Congressmen from

123. Barone et al., *Almanac of American Politics*, p. 53. Mailliard was given a safer district in the 1972 line drawing.
124. On member freedom see Bauer et al., *American Business and Public Policy*, pp. 406–07.

the traditional parts of old machine cities rarely advertise and seldom take positions on anything (except on roll calls), but devote a great deal of time and energy to the distribution of benefits. In fact they use their office resources to plug themselves into their local party organizations. Congressman William A. Barrett (D., downtown Philadelphia), chairman of the Housing Subcommittee of the House Banking and Currency Committee, claimed in 1971 to have spent only three nights in Washington in the preceding six years. He meets constituents each night from 9:00 P.M. to 1:00 A.M. in the home district; "Folks line up to tell Bill Barrett their problems." [125] On the other hand congressmen with upper-middle-class bases (suburban, city reform, or academic) tend to deal in positions. In New York City the switch from regular to reform Democrats is a switch from members who emphasize benefits to members who emphasize positions; it reflects a shift in consumer taste.[126] The same dif-

125. Linda M. Kupferstein, Nader profile on William A. Barrett (D., Pa.), p. 1. This profile gives a very useful account of a machine congressman's activities.

126. One commentator on New York detects "a tendency for the media to promote what may be termed 'press release politicians.'" A result is that "younger members tend to gravitate towards House committees that have high rhetorical and perhaps symbolic importance, like Foreign Affairs and Government Operations, rather than those with bread-and-butter payoffs." Donald Haider, "The New York City Congressional Delegation," *City Almanac* (published bimonthly by the Center for New York City

ference appears geographically rather than temporally as one goes from the inner wards to the outer suburbs of Chicago.[127]

Another kind of difference appears if the initial assumption of a reelection quest is relaxed to take into account the "progressive" ambitions of some members —the aspirations of some to move up to higher electoral offices rather than keep the ones they have.[128] There are two important subsets of climbers in the Congress—House members who would like to be senators (over the years about a quarter of the senators have come up directly from the House),[129] and senators who would like to be presidents or vice presidents (in the Ninety-third Congress about a quarter of the senators had at one time or another run for these offices or been seriously "mentioned" for them). In both cases higher aspirations seem to produce the same distinctive mix of activities. For one thing credit claiming is all but useless. It does little good to talk

Affairs of the New School for Social Research), vol. 7, no. 6, April 1973, p. 11.

127. Snowiss, "Congressional Recruitment and Representation."

128. The term is from Joseph A. Schlesinger, *Ambition and Politics: Political Careers in the United States* (Chicago: Rand McNally, 1966), p. 10.

129. Ibid., p. 92; Matthews, *U.S. Senators*, p. 55. In the years 1953–72 three House members were appointed to the Senate, and eighty-five gave up their seats to run for the Senate. Thirty-five of the latter made it, giving a success rate of 41 percent.

about the bacon you have brought back to a district you are trying to abandon. And, as Lyndon Johnson found in 1960, claiming credit on legislative maneuvers is no way to reach a new mass audience; it baffles rather than persuades. Office advancement seems to require a judicious mixture of advertising and position taking. Thus a House member aiming for the Senate heralds his quest with press releases; there must be a new "image," sometimes an ideological overhaul to make ready for the new constituency.[130] Senators aiming for the White House do more or less the same thing—advertising to get the name across, position taking ("We can do better"). In recent years presidential aspirants have sought Foreign Relations Committee membership as a platform for making statements on foreign policy.[131]

There are these distinctions, but it would be a mistake to elevate them over the commonalities. For most congressmen most of the time all three activities are essential. This closing vignette of Senator Strom Thurmond (R., S.C.) making his peace with universal suffrage is a good picture of what the electoral side of

130. Thus upstate New York Republicans moving to the Senate commonly shift to the left. For a good example of the advertising and position-taking strategies that can go along with turning a House member into a senator see the account on Senator Robert P. Griffin (R., Mich.) in James M. Perry, *The New Politics* (New York: Clarkson N. Potter, 1968), ch. 4.

131. Fenno, *Congressmen in Committees*, pp. 141–42.

American legislative politics is all about. The senator was reacting in 1971 to a 1970 Democratic gubernatorial victory in his state in which black turnout was high:

Since then, the Republican Senator has done the following things:

—Hired Thomas Moss, a black political organizer who directed Negro voter registration efforts for the South Carolina Voter Education Project, for his staff in South Carolina, and a black secretary for his Washington office.

—Announced Federal grants for projects in black areas, including at least one occasion when he addressed a predominantly black audience to announce a rural water project and remained afterwards to shake hands.

—Issued moderate statements on racial issues.

In a statement to Ebony magazine that aides say Thurmond wrote himself, he said, "In most instances I am confident that we have more in common as Southerners than we have reason to oppose each other because of race. Equality of opportunity for all is a goal upon which blacks and Southern whites can agree." [132]

132. "Thurmond Image Seen as Changing," *New York Times*, October 17, 1971, p. 46.

2

PROCESSES AND POLICIES

We live in a cocoon of good feeling—no doubt the compensation for the cruel buffeting that is received in the world outside.

—a comment by the late Clem Miller (D., Calif.) on serving in the House

The purpose of part 1 of this essay was to show what activities are electorally useful to congressmen. The goal of part 2 will be to show what happens when members who need to engage in these activities assemble for collective action. The argument will be long and complicated, with some backing and filling, but with this general ordering of subjects: first, an examination of the salient structural units of Congress (offices, committees, parties) and the ways in which these units are arranged to meet electoral needs; second, an exploration of the "functions" Congress fulfills or is thought to fulfill; third, an examination of structural arrangements in Congress that serve the end of institutional maintenance; fourth, a discussion of the place of assemblies in governance in the United States and elsewhere; and fifth, a consideration of "reform" efforts provoked by dissatisfaction with congressional performance.

It will be useful to start here with two prefatory points—to be substantiated as the discussion proceeds. The first is that the organization of Congress meets remarkably well the electoral needs of its members. To put it another way, if a group of planners sat down and tried to design a pair of American national assemblies with the goal of serving members' electoral needs year in and year out, they would be hard pressed to improve on what exists. The second point is that satisfaction of electoral needs requires remarkably little zero-sum conflict among members. That is, one member's gain is not another member's loss; to a remarkable degree members can successfully engage in electorally useful activities without denying other members the opportunity successfully to engage in them. In regard to credit claiming, this second point requires elaboration further on. Its application to advertising is perhaps obvious. The members all have different markets, so that what any one member does is not an inconvenience to any other. There are exceptions here—House members are sometimes thrown into districts together, senators have to watch the advertising of ambitious House members within their states, and senators from the same state have to keep up with each other[1]—but the case generally holds. With position taking the point is also reasonably clear. As long as congressmen do not attack each other—and

1. "Each senator watches the publicity of his colleague very closely indeed, and many a feud has been touched off by the fact that one senator seemed to be getting better publicity than the other. Sometimes full-scale 'publicity battles' will break out between the two senators. . . . The relations between two senators from the same state are almost always strained, and their competition for publicity in the same arena seems to be one reason for this coolness." Matthews, *U.S. Senators*, p. 216. It may be that the problem is especially acute when two senators are members of the same party with similar supporting coalitions. Senator Douglas

they rarely do[2]—any member can champion the most extraordinary causes without inconveniencing any of his colleagues. The *Congressional Record* is largely a series of disjointed insertions prepared for the eyes of relevant political actors, with each member enjoying final editing rights on his materials.[3]

recalls from his days in office that Senator Jacob Javits (R., N.Y.) had "a genius for hitting the front page of the New York *Times* and *Herald Tribune* every morning. The rivalry for newspaper attention between Jack and his Republican colleague, Kenneth Keating, was both intense and amusing. When one would make a brief and catching statement on the floor during the morning hour, the other would soon rush in to deliver another speech on the same topic, but with a different twist." *In the Fullness of Time*, p. 248.

2. A congressional norm easily arrived at and well ingrained is that members should not attack each other—even across party lines. "Public disparagement of colleagues is strongly discouraged; it is not the way to play the game. Personal attacks are sharply censured, and members seldom invade the congressional districts of colleagues of another party to campaign against them. Democrats reacted strongly to the action of one House Republican in sending letters into the district of a Democratic colleague criticizing the latter for apparent inconsistencies between a stated position and a vote." Clapp, *The Congressman*, pp. 16–17. See also Matthews, *U.S. Senators*, pp. 97–99. These references are to personal attacks. Militant disagreement between members "on the issues" can of course be helpful to both sides if the constituencies differ.

3. Editing rights are carefully protected. See Roger H. Davidson, David M. Kovenock, and Michael K. O'Leary, *Congress in Crisis* (Belmont, Calif.: Wadsworth, 1966), p. 118. The *Record* was more or less the same a century ago. See Woodrow Wilson, *Congressional Government* (New York: Meridian, 1960), p. 76.

A scrutiny of the basic structural units of Congress will yield evidence to support both these prefatory points. First, there are the 535 Capitol Hill *offices,* the small personal empires of the members. Annual staff salary schedules now run at about $150,000 per office on the House side, with variation upward according to state population on the Senate side. The Hill office is a vitally important political unit, part campaign management firm and part political machine. The availability of its staff members for election work in and out of season gives it some of the properties of the former; its casework capabilities, some of the properties of the latter. And there is the franking privilege for use on office emanations. The dollar value of this array of resources in an election campaign is difficult to estimate. Leuthold gives a 1962 value of $25,000 for House members (including a sum for member salary).[4] In 1971 a House member put it at $100,000 (including a sum for general media exposure).[5] The value has certainly increased over the last decade. It should be said that the availability of these incumbency advantages causes little displeasure among members. In the early 1970s a flurry of court decisions brought the franking privilege under attack. The reaction of the House was to pass a bill outlawing some of the more

4. Leuthold, *Electioneering in a Democracy,* p. 131.
5. Richard Harris, "Annals of Politics: A Fundamental Hoax," *New Yorker,* July 7, 1971, p. 48.

questionable uses but also rendering the frank less vulnerable to judicial incursion. The spirit of the reform was evident in a statement of the bill's floor manager: "The fact is that 98 or 99 percent of the material going out of the mail room is good, solid information and in the public interest." [6] A final comment on congressional offices is perhaps the most important one: office resources are given to all members regardless of party, seniority, or any other qualification. They come with the job.

Second among the structural units are the *committees*, the twenty-one standing committees in the House and seventeen in the Senate—with a scattering of other special and joint bodies.[7] Committee membership can be electorally useful in a number of different ways. Some committees supply good platforms for position taking. The best example over the years is probably the House Un-American Activities Committee (now the Internal Security Committee), whose members have displayed hardly a trace of an interest in legislation.[8] Lowi has a chart showing numbers of days devoted to HUAC public hearings in Congresses from

6. *Congressional Record* (daily ed.), April 11, 1973, p. H2601. The floor manager was Morris Udall (D., Ariz.).

7. The more interesting characteristics of the House Rules, Ways and Means, and Appropriations committees will be left for treatment later under institutional maintenance.

8. The best account of HUAC activities is in Walter Goodman, *The Committee* (New York: Farrar, Straus and Giroux, 1968).

the Eightieth through the Eighty-ninth. It can be read as a supply chart, showing biennial volume of position taking on subversion and related matters; by inference it can also be read as a measure of popular demand (the peak years were 1949–56).[9] Senator Joseph McCarthy used the Senate Government Operations Committee as his investigative base in the Eighty-third Congress; later on in the 1960s Senators Abraham Ribicoff (D., Conn.) and William Proxmire (D., Wis.) used subcommittees of this same unit in catching public attention respectively on auto safety and defense waste.[10] With membership on the Senate Foreign Relations Committee goes a license to make speeches on foreign policy.[11] Some committees perhaps deserve to be designated "cause committees"; membership on them can confer an ostentatious identification with salient public causes. An example is the House Educa-

9. Theodore J. Lowi, *The Politics of Disorder* (New York: Basic Books, 1971), p. 117. Shils had this assessment of the investigations of the late 1940s: "The congressional investigation is often just the instrument which the legislator needs in order to remind his constituents of his existence. That is the reason why investigations often involve such unseemly uses of the organs of publicity. Publicity is the next best thing to the personal contact which the legislator must forego. It is his substitute offering by which he tries to counteract the personal contact which his rivals at home have with the constituents." Edward A. Shils, "Congressional Investigations: The Legislator and His Environment," 18 *University of Chicago Law Review* 573 (1950–51).

10. On Ribicoff see David Price, *Who Makes the Laws?*, p. 50.

11. See Fenno, *Congressmen in Committees*, p. 189.

tion and Labor Committee, whose members, in Fenno's analysis, have two "strategic premises": "to prosecute policy partisanship" and "to pursue one's individual policy preferences regardless of party." [12] Committee members do a good deal of churning about on education, poverty, and similar matters. In recent years Education and Labor has attracted media-conscious members such as Shirley Chisholm (D., N.Y.), Herman Badillo (D., N.Y.), and Louise Day Hicks (D., Mass.).[13]

Some committees traffic in particularized benefits. Just how benefits of this sort are likely to be distributed by governments has been the subject of theoretical speculation. Buchanan and Tullock suggest a kind of round-robin rip-off model, with seriatim majorities coalescing to do in excluded minorities.[14] Barry replies

12. Ibid., pp. 75–76.

13. Fenno assigns his House members three basic goals: (1) having more influence inside the House than other congressmen, (2) helping their constituents and thereby insuring their reelection, and (3) helping to make good public policy. Ibid., ch. 1. The second of these evokes what here has been called credit-claiming behavior. Fenno puts his Education and Labor members in the third category. But he has no place for position taking, and indeed it is doubtful whether position taking is the sort of activity that would make a vivid and explicit appearance in interview data. It is probably more useful to watch what members do than what they say they intend to do, and on the actual activities of Education and Labor members Fenno's account is fascinating and persuasive. Ibid., pp. 85–88, 101–05, 127–33, 226–42. More on the committee later.

14. Buchanan and Tullock, *The Calculus of Consent*, pp. 135–40.

that politicians who have to deal with each other over time are more likely to come up with an "obvious solution" that more securely protects their interests.[15] The congressional evidence is overwhelmingly with Barry. Specifically, in giving out particularized benefits where the costs are diffuse (falling on taxpayer or consumer) and where in the long run to reward one congressman is not obviously to deprive others,[16] the members follow a policy of universalism.[17] That is, every member, regardless of party or seniority, has a right to his share of benefits. There is evidence of universalism in the distribution of projects on House

15. Brian Barry, *Political Argument* (London: Routledge and Kegan Paul, 1965), pp. 255–56. "It would require trust, but hardly altruism, for all concerned to settle on some scheme from which all would benefit compared with the alternatives of deadlock or anarchy." p. 253.

16. There can be controversy, of course, over specific benefits. If only one federal office building is to be built in the Midwest it cannot simultaneously be put in Des Moines and Omaha. But over time office buildings are the sorts of goods that can be given out in fair shares. Another kind of problem arises with pre-1934 tariff bargaining, a game not all congressmen were in a position to play. But the evidence is that most of the time all who wanted to play were dealt in (e.g. Pennsylvania and Louisiana Democrats). Members who had no protectable products suffered no political deprivation, for they could fall back on militant antitariff position taking.

17. In Polsby's treatment of the House, this is one of the properties of an "institutionalized" organization. Polsby, "Institutionalization of the House," p. 145.

Public Works,[18] projects on House Interior,[19] projects on Senate Interior,[20] project money on House Appropriations,[21] project money on Senate Appropriations,[22] tax benefits on House Ways and Means,[23] tax benefits on Senate Finance,[24] and (by inference from the reported data) urban renewal projects on House Banking and Currency.[25] The House Interior Committee, in Fenno's account, "takes as its major decision rule a determination to process and pass *all* requests and to do so in such a way as to maximize the chances of passage in the House. Succinctly, then, Interior's major strategic premise is: *to secure House passage of all*

18. Murphy, "House Public Works Committee," pp. 3, 23, 39.

19. Fenno, *Congressmen in Committees*, p. 58.

20. Ibid., pp. 165–66.

21. Fenno, *Power of the Purse*, pp. 85–87.

22. Fenno, *Congressmen in Committees*, p. 160; Stephen Horn, *Unused Power: The Work of the Senate Committee on Appropriations* (Washington, D.C.: Brookings, 1970), p. 91.

23. Manley, *The Politics of Finance*, pp. 78–84; Surrey, "Congress and the Tax Lobbyist."

24. Fenno, *Congressmen in Committees*, pp. 156–59; Surrey, "Congress and the Tax Lobbyist." Depletion allowances offer a good example of universalism. Initial allowances for products like oil provoked appeals for more esoteric ones like rock asphalt and ball and sagger clay. "Since 1942, the list of tax-favored minerals has become all-encompassing, and there is likely not a single state without its own built-in pro-depletion lobby." Stern, *Rape of the Taxpayer*, p. 298.

25. Charles R. Plott, "Some Organizational Influences on Urban Renewal Decisions," 58 *American Economic Review* 306–11 (May 1968).

constituency-supported, Member-sponsored bills." [26] House
Public Works, writes Murphy, has a "norm of mutual
advantage"; in the words of one of its members, "[We]
have a rule on the Committee, it's not a rule of the
Committee, it's not written down or anything, but it's
just the way we do things. Any time any member of
the Committee wants something, or wants to get a bill
out, we get it out for him. . . . Makes no difference—
Republican or Democrat. We are all Americans when
it comes to that." [27] Not surprisingly there is some
evidence that members of these distributive committees gain more from them than nonmembers.[28] But
there is also evidence that committee members act as
procurers for others in their states or regions.[29] An
interesting aspect of particularistic politics is its special
brand of "rules." There have to be allocation guidelines precise enough to admit judgments on benefit
"soundness" (no member can have everything he
wants), yet ambiguous enough to allow members to

26. Fenno, *Congressmen in Committees*, p. 58.

27. Murphy, "House Public Works Committee," p. 23.

28. See, for example, Plott, "Organizational Influences on
Urban Renewal Decisions"; and also Carol F. Goss, "Military
Committee Membership and Defense-Related Benefits in the
House of Representatives," 25 *Western Political Quarterly* 215–33
(1972).

29. See, for example, Murphy, "House Public Works Committee," p. 8; Fenno, *Power of the Purse*, pp. 87–88; Fenno, *Congressmen
in Committees*, pp. 272–73; Barbara Deckard, "State Party Delegations in the United States House of Representatives—An Analysis
of Group Action," 5 *Polity* 327–33 (1973).

claim personal credit for what they get. Hence there
are unending policy minuets; an example is the one in
public works where the partners are the Corps of
Army Engineers with its cost-benefit calculations and
the congressmen with their ad hoc exceptions.[30]

Particularism also has its position-taking side. On
occasion members capture public attention by de-
nouncing the allocation process itself; thus in 1972 a
number of liberals held up some Ways and Means
"members' bills" on the House floor.[31] But such efforts
have little or no effect. Senator Douglas used to offer
floor amendments to excise projects from public works
appropriations bills, but he had a hard time even
getting the Senate to vote on them.[32]

30. See Murphy, "House Public Works Committee," pp. 39–47;
and also Arthur Maass, *Muddy Waters: The Army Engineers and the
Nation's Rivers* (Cambridge: Harvard University Press, 1951), ch. 1.
In the late years of the congressional tariff there was a set of
allocation guidelines based on differences between home and
foreign production costs of individual products. The economics of
all this was decidedly dubious, and the cost figures were virtually
nonexistent. But the idea was politically serviceable. See
Schattschneider, *Politics, Pressures, and the Tariff*, pp. 67–84.

31. Eileen Shanahan, "Special Tax Bills Blocked by Reform
Drive in House," *New York Times*, March 1, 1972, p. 1.

32. Douglas, *In the Fullness of Time*, pp. 269–70, 314–18. "Other
members of the Senate had little to gain and everything to lose by
supporting a specific cut, and so they had no incentive to stay on
the floor to vote. As a result, although I tried for ten years to make
cuts, always with a thorough case, I was constantly beaten. Often I
failed to get the necessary one-fifth for a quorum roll call, and even
if I did, I was overwhelmingly defeated." P. 315. Senator James L.
Buckley (R., N.Y.), following in the Douglas tradition, recently

Finally, and very importantly, the committee system aids congressmen simply by allowing a division of labor among members. The parceling out of legislation among small groups of congressmen by subject area has two effects. First, it creates small voting bodies in which membership may be valuable. An attentive interest group will prize more highly the favorable issue positions of members of committees pondering its fortunes than the favorable positions of the general run of congressmen. Second, it creates specialized small-group settings in which individual congressmen can make things happen and be perceived to make things happen. "I put that bill through committee." "That was my amendment." "I talked them around on that." This is the language of credit claiming. It comes easily in the committee setting and also when "expert" committee members handle bills on the floor. To attentive audiences it can be believable. Some political actors follow committee activities closely and mobilize electoral resources to support deserving members.[33]

---

tried to delete forty-four public works projects at the committee stage in the Senate. The members voted down all his amendments except the ones cutting out projects in New York; these latter they adopted. See Richard Reeves, "Isn't It Time We Had a Senator?", *New York*, February 25, 1974, p. 38.

33. For about a decade there have been enough published data to allow statistical analyses of the strategies groups use in giving campaign money to congressional candidates. No one has done any. Three strategies are detectable. Some outfits—the AFL-CIO Committee on Political Education is an example—follow a

The postal unions have been mentioned. In the late 1960s the tobacco industry got together a campaign kitty to finance House Commerce Committee members who had been taking a position against tobacco labeling.[34] In 1970 BANKPAC, a bankers' outfit, distributed money among members of the House Banking and Currency Committee.[35] In his 1970 campaign Congressman George H. Fallon (D., Md.), chairman of the House Public Works Committee, received 167 donations from highway-construction interests in thirty-seven states other than his own.[36] Also in 1970 a group representing cable-television interests gave $1,000 to the Committee for Effective Government, an outfit set up solely to back the campaign of Congressman Torbert H. Macdonald,

"marginal-ideological" strategy; that is, they give funds to candidates of a particular ideological view, and they concentrate money in the marginal states and districts. The official Democratic and Republican campaign committees of the House seem to follow a "fair shares" strategy; that is, they divide up money more or less equally among their incumbents. And some groups (including some referred to below in the text) follow an "interest" strategy; that is, they give money to members of particular committees, with little regard for party affiliation, and with higher contributions going to senior members who are usually in rather safe districts.

34. Jerry Landauer, "Political Fund-Raising: A Murky World," *Wall Street Journal*, June 28, 1967, p. 14.

35. Walter Pincus, "Silent Spenders in Politics: They Really Give at the Office," *New York*, January 31, 1972, pp. 42–43.

36. Harris, "Annals of Politics," p. 52. Fallon still managed to lose his primary.

chairman of the Communications and Power Subcommittee of the House Commerce Committee.[37] Money, of course, is only one electoral resource among many. With the postal unions volunteer work was probably more useful. But money is an important resource, and it can be used in sophisticated fashion by good committee watchers.[38]

A list of the standing committees only begins to show the congressional division of labor. At the beginning of the Ninety-third Congress there were 143 subcommittees in the Senate and 132 in the House.[39] With disaggregation carried to this extreme the number of members covering subject areas becomes small enough to permit relatively easy credit claiming. Thus

37. Ibid.

38. "For example, at the Washington headquarters of the National Small Business Association . . . a computer operation has been set up to make the most of the money its members have donated to members of Congress. When a bill that the association is interested in comes up in committee, a specific list of who gave how much to which members of the committee is produced by the computer. Workers in the headquarters then telephone donors— often men with wide influence, since they usually sit on boards of directors of various companies and can call on those connections, too—and ask them to get in touch with the member, or members, of the committee they helped, and remind them of the association's position on the legislation in question. That way, only eight or ten members of a committee, rather than a majority of the House members, have to be reached." Ibid., p. 56.

39. As listed in _Congressional Quarterly Weekly_, April 28, 1973. There were also sixteen subcommittees of the joint committees.

on the House Agriculture Committee there are no
more than about half a dozen members handling each
commodity.[40] In small working units formal voting
tends to recede in importance as a determinant of
outcome, and what individual members do with their
time and energy rises in importance. Whatever else it
may be, the quest for specialization in Congress is a
quest for credit. Every member can aspire to occupy a
part of at least one piece of policy turf small enough so
that he can claim personal responsibility for some of
the things that happen on it.[41] Better yet, he can aspire
to rise in seniority and claim ever more responsibility
—perhaps even be christened a "czar" or a "baron"
by the press.[42] What the congressional seniority system

40. Charles O. Jones, "The Role of the Congressional Subcommittee," 6 *Midwest Journal of Political Science* 327–44 (1962).

41. Price supplies a good example of an occupier of policy turf
in his writing on Senator Warren Magnuson (D., Wash.):
"Shipping and fishing . . . were areas in which Magnuson had
been interested since he first came to Congress in 1937. They were
important to [the state of] Washington, and the groups involved
wielded considerable influence there and controlled sizable campaign chests. As Magnuson gained seniority and influence, he was
increasingly in a position to champion the interests of American
shipping and fishing; his assumption of that role worked to his and
industry's mutual advantage." David Price, *Who Makes the Laws?*,
p. 63.

42. See, for example, Norman C. Miller, "The Farm Baron:
Rep. Jamie Whitten [D., Miss.] Works behind Scenes to Shape Big
Spending," *Wall Street Journal*, June 7, 1971, p. 1. Whitten is
chairman of the Subcommittee on Agriculture of the House
Appropriations Committee.

old boy
variety

does as a system is to convert turf into property; it assures a congressman that once he initially occupies a piece of turf, no one can ever push him off it. And the property automatically appreciates in value over time. With these advantages for all hands, it is not surprising that congressmen are strongly attached to the seniority system.[43]

In recent years there have been efforts to reform seniority in the House, and in fact both parties have changed some of their rules. But the problem here seems to be not that members are against the system but that there is not enough turf to go around. House members are staying on the Hill longer, with the result that there are more members who have lasted several terms and who feel entitled to wield considerable subcommittee influence. The reform drive has produced a devolution (in some committees) of staff and budget resources to the subcommittee level, and a Democratic rule that no member can hold more than one subcommittee chairmanship.[44] But the House may

43. In the Eighty-eighth Congress House members were polled to find out their positions on thirty-two proposals for reforming the House. The proposal with least support (14 percent "strongly for" or "for," 86 percent "strongly against" or "against") was one to "require members to forfeit seniority privileges after each six consecutive terms." (The only proposal with a majority "strongly for" it was one to allot more money for staff salaries.) Davidson et al., *Congress in Crisis*, app. B. In the Senate, writes Matthews, the seniority system "is almost universally approved." Matthews, *U.S. Senators*, p. 163.

44. "Thus structural reform in Congress is generally a product of those who feel shortchanged when it comes to power. . . . The

have to create more subcommittees to satisfy its members. There is little reform impetus in the Senate, where there are more subcommittees than there are senators.

The other basic structural units in Congress are the *parties*. The case here will be that the parties, like the offices and committees, are tailored to suit members' electoral needs. They are more useful for what they are not than for what they are. It is easy to conjure up visions of the sorts of zero-sum politics parties could import into a representative assembly. One possibility —in line with the analysis here—is that a majority party could deprive minority members of a share of particularized benefits, a share of committee influence, and a share of resources to advertise and make their positions known. Congressional majorities obviously do not shut out minorities in this fashion. It would make no sense to do so; the costs of cutting in minority

reason that major reform efforts of the 1960s and 1970s have emanated from the liberal Democrats is simply that they were most in need of payoffs." Norman J. Ornstein, "Causes and Consequences of Congressional Change: Subcommittee Reforms in the House of Representatives, 1970–1973," paper presented to the annual convention of the American Political Science Association, 1973, p. 1. A point that should be kept in mind is that some subcommittees are useful as bases for position taking—with hearings, investigations, and such. This may be the consequence of a recent proliferation of chairmanships on the House Foreign Affairs Committee. See Fenno, *Congressmen in Committees*, pp. 283–85.

members are very low, whereas the costs of losing majority control in a cutthroat partisan politics of this kind would be very high.[45] A more conventional zero-sum vision is the one in which assembly parties organize in disciplined fashion for the purpose of enacting general party "programs"; the battle is over whose program shall prevail. It should be obvious that if they wanted to, American congressmen could immediately and permanently array themselves in disciplined legions for the purpose of programmatic combat. They do not. Every now and then a member does emit a Wilsonian call for program and cohesion,[46] but

45. Discrimination of this sort might also be a recipe for civil war, and it is doubtful whether many assemblies anywhere engage in it. Where assemblies have important decision powers, a pattern of militant position taking on the floor combined with amiable particularistic logrolling and interest-group servicing in committee seems a common one. It is a design for spreading contentment among an entire membership. Thus in the Italian parliament Communist deputies seem to get their share of particularistic benefits, and they seem to have little trouble working with Christian Democrats at the committee level. See Georgio Galli and Alfonso Prandi, *Patterns of Political Participation in Italy* (New Haven: Yale University Press, 1970), pp. 268–74.

46. In the plan of Congressman Richard Bolling (D., Mo.), "The party leader would become the true leader of a legislative team that would produce a coherent and co-ordinated legislative program." Bolling, *House Out of Order* (New York: Dutton, 1965), p. 241. Former Senator Joseph Clark (D., Pa.) puts forth this objective: "To change the party leadership structure so that within both parties and in both houses a majority will decide party policy and enforce party discipline against recalcitrant members." Clark,

these exhortations fail to arouse much member interest. The fact is that the enactment of party programs is electorally not very important to members (although some may find it important to take positions on programs).

What is important to each congressman, and vitally so, is that he be free to take positions that serve his advantage.[47] There is no member of either house who would not be politically injured—or at least who would not think he would be injured—by being made to toe a party line on all policies (unless of course he could determine the line). There is no congressional bloc whose members have identical position needs across all issues. Thus on the school bussing issue in the Ninety-second Congress, it was vital to Detroit white liberal Democratic House members that they be free to vote one way and to Detroit black liberal Democrats that they be free to vote the other. In regard to these member needs the best service a party can supply

---

Congress: The Sapless Branch (New York: Harper and Row, 1964), p. 166.

47. Cf. Huitt on party platforms: "The attitude of the member of Congress toward the platform is precisely the same as that of the President: he uses it, condemns it, or ignores it as it suits him in dealing with *his* constituency. . . . The constituency has a virtually unqualified power to hire and fire. If the member pleases it, no party leader can fatally hurt him; if he does not, no national party organization can save him." Ralph K. Huitt, "Democratic Party Leadership in the Senate," ch. 3 in Huitt and Peabody, *Congress*, p. 140.

to its congressmen is a negative one; it can leave them alone. And this in general is what the congressional parties do. Party leaders are chosen not to be program salesmen or vote mobilizers, but to be brokers, favor-doers, agenda-setters, and protectors of established institutional routines.[48] Party "pressure" to vote one way or another is minimal.[49] Party "whipping" hardly deserves the name.[50] Leaders in both houses have a

48. See Nelson W. Polsby, "Two Strategies of Influence: Choosing a Majority Leader, 1962," ch. 3 in Peabody and Polsby, *New Perspectives on the House*; and Robert L. Peabody, "The Selection of a Majority Leader, 1970–71: The Democratic Caucus and Its Aftermath," unpublished manuscript.

49. "Many new members of the House express surprise that so little pressure is exerted by the party leadership regarding voting. Clearly they had anticipated more frequent guidance or instruction. Their more senior colleagues also indicate that leadership intervention is minimal. Activities of the party whips prior to a vote generally consist of little more than perfunctory requests to be on the floor or occasional checks regarding the intended vote of the member. Seldom is advice given or party position urged." Clapp, *The Congressman*, p. 150.

50. Froman and Ripley report data on polls the House Democratic whip's office took in 1963 to find out how members stood on upcoming bills. The office took soundings on only ten bills, and the predictions on whether or how members would vote were correct in only 90.5 percent of cases. A 10 percent error rate! Party leaders work in a context in which member positions are pretty well fixed, and in which it is surprisingly difficult to figure out what they are. Lewis A. Froman and Randall B. Ripley, "Conditions for Party Leadership: The Case of the House Democrats," 59 *American Political Science Review* 54 (1965). One problem is that some Democratic assistant whips are unenthusiastic about party causes.

habit of counseling members to "vote their constituencies." The Senate Democratic whip, Robert C. Byrd (D., W. Va.), studies the voting records of his members, and when they appear on the floor for a roll call, he "tries to steer them in their own direction with a 'this is a no (or yes) for you.' " [51] In fact neither congressional party demands anything like a truth test of its members. Anyone who survives a Democratic (or Republican) primary and a November election is entitled to appear in Washington and proclaim himself a Democratic (or Republican) congressman. Wild heresy can pose some problems—a Republican liberal would find it difficult to win an appointment to the Ways and Means Committee. Even so, a member can build a quite satisfactory career within either congressional party regardless of his issue positions. As time goes on, the seniority system protects him from party incursion.[52] The issue catholicity of the congressional

See Randall B. Ripley, "The Party Whip Organizations in the United States House of Representatives," 58 *American Political Science Review* 569 (1964).

51. Paul R. Wieck, "Keeping Senate Traffic Moving: The Efficiency Byrd," *New Republic*, January 20, 1973, p. 13. See also Clapp, *The Congressman*, p. 288. Byrd achieved his position by being a good favor-doer. "Byrd's strength in the Senate is made up of his loyalty to the club, his thoughtfulness or sycophancy (depending on your perspective), his willingness to do the drudgery and take care of the details." Sherrill, "Poor White Power," p. 52.

52. In recent years House Democrats have deprived three members of their seniority for endorsing presidential candidates of

parties probably accounts for the fact that hardly any congressmen serve as independents or members of third parties. With no admissions standards it is easy enough for everyone to be a Democrat or a Republican.[53]

Of course the congressional parties are still important pieces of Capitol Hill furniture. There remain significant differences between Democrats and Republicans in their roll call voting.[54] Partisan electoral

---

other parties. But this new standard poses no threat to incumbents who want to keep their seniority. It is astonishingly easy to refrain from endorsing presidential candidates of other parties.

53. When compared with assemblies in other countries (even the English-speaking countries) the American Congress is exceptional in its lack of minor party members. See the discussion in Douglas Rae, *The Political Consequences of Electoral Laws* (New Haven: Yale University Press, 1967), p. 141. The proportion of the House popular vote cast for minor party candidates has declined during this century—from figures usually in the 4 to 6 percent range in 1896–1920, to figures in the 2 to 4 percent range in 1920–42, to figures generally under 2 percent after 1942. See Gerald H. Kramer and Susan J. Lepper, "Congressional Elections," ch. 5 in William O. Aydelotte et al., *The Dimensions of Quantitative Research in History* (Princeton: Princeton University Press, 1972), pp. 264–65. The decline is probably a consequence of the adoption of the direct primary system at the state level. The primary gives each of the major parties a great deal of issue flexibility at the nominating stage. Any popular cause can find expression in a major party, and any politician, regardless of his views, can try to win a major party nomination.

54. For recent treatments see Clausen, *How Congressmen Decide*; Julius Turner, *Party and Constituency: Pressures on Congress* (Baltimore: Johns Hopkins Press, 1970 edition revised by Edward V. Schneier,

swings, by taking out members sustained by one kind of supporting coalition and bringing in members sustained by another, can change the position-taking balance in both houses with detectable legislative effect (as in the Eightieth and Eighty-ninth Congresses). The custom of denying committee and subcommittee chairmanships to minority party members remains one of the two leading forms of invidious discrimination on the Hill (the other being discrimination by seniority). Yet as time goes on, all this adds up to less and less. "Party voting" in the House, however defined, has been declining since the turn of the century and has reached a record low in the last decade.[55] Partisan seat swings in the House have declined considerably in amplitude; one reason is that a fall in the proportion of incumbents holding seats in the marginal range has lowered the casualty rate in times of voter volatility.[56] Alternation in party control

Jr.); David R. Mayhew, *Party Loyalty among Congressmen* (Cambridge: Harvard University Press, 1966).

55. Turner, *Party and Constituency*, ch. 2. In this 1970 updating of the 1951 Turner work, Schneier writes, "By comparison with Julius Turner's original *Party and Constituency*, the single most striking finding of this study is the continuing decline of party voting in the House of Representatives." P. 239. Probably what has been going on here is that politicians have come to rely on party cues less as the information explosion has made other cues available (e.g. cues from polling data).

56. See Mayhew, "Congressional Elections." Tufte defines a "swing ratio"—a "rate of translation of votes into seats"—that

has at least temporarily ceased, with the Democrats becoming something of a "party of state" at the congressional level; in both houses unbroken Democratic control in the years 1955–74 has set durability records unmatched since the rise of the two-party system in the 1830s. As for chairmanship discrimination against Republicans, it is made bearable by the fact that minority members on most committees share in the decision making in all its stages.[57] Some committees look like dual (limited) monarchies, with Democratic chairman and ranking Republican congenially sharing influence. Among the notable partnerships of recent years have been those of J. W. Fulbright (D., Ark.) and George D. Aiken (R., Vt.) on Senate Foreign Relations, Wilbur D. Mills (D., Ark.) and John W. Byrnes (R., Wis.) on House Ways and Means, and Emanuel Celler (D., N.Y.) and William M. McCulloch (R., Ohio) on House Judiciary.[58] The general picture of the congressional party system is one

---

yields an exceptionally low United States House reading for the late 1960s. Edward R. Tufte, "The Relationship between Seats and Votes in Two-Party Systems," 67 *American Political Science Review* 550 (1973).

57. There are records of minority exclusion in the past. In the 1920s the fifteen Ways and Means Republicans used to mark up tariff bills by themselves. See F. W. Taussig, *The Tariff History of the United States* (New York: G. P. Putnam's Sons, 1931), p. 492. When the Republicans came blustering back into power in the Eightieth Congress, they used steamroller tactics against the Democratic minority on the House Appropriations Committee. See Fenno, *Power of the Purse*, pp. 245–49.

58. Yet there does remain the discrimination. One wonders what kinds of linkage theories can still be conjured up to justify it.

of a system in slow decline—or, to put it another way, a system whose zero-sum edges have been eroded away by powerful norms of institutional universalism. In a good many ways the interesting division in congressional politics is not between Democrats and Republicans, but between politicians in and out of office. Looked at from one angle the cult of universalism has the appearance of a cross-party conspiracy among incumbents to keep their jobs.[59]

Committee chairmen working together to put across a party program? No such thing. Party slates of chairmen differentiated by devotion to separate sets of party principles? Very dubious. Alternation in control between slates of chairmen? There is none. What lingers on is a sort of demographic discrimination.

59. One place where universalism prevails over party division is in House districting. Wherever congressmen have a say on line drawing, they seem to prefer cross-party deals among members of a state delegation assuring safe seats for all incumbents. For an account of the California districting of 1967 see Joseph W. Sullivan, "Massive Gerrymander Mapped in California by 38 Congressmen," *Wall Street Journal*, November 9, 1967, p. 1. For an account of the incumbency plan proposed by the Illinois delegation for 1972 see "Redistricting: Intervention of U.S. Court in Illinois," *Congressional Quarterly Weekly*, October 23, 1971, pp. 2180–85. "Most of the [Illinois] Republican incumbents preferred a map that cost the party a chance to win three seats but preserved their own districts virtually intact." P. 2181. For a general discussion see David R. Mayhew, "Congressional Representation: Theory and Practice in Drawing the Districts," ch. 7 in Nelson W. Polsby (ed.), *Reapportionment in the 1970's* (Berkeley: University of California Press, 1971), pp. 274–84.

With congressmen having the electoral needs they do, and with congressional institutions tailored to suit these needs in the foregoing ways, what happens? What are the policy consequences of these arrangements? A traditional route to an answer takes the form of a rundown of functions performed by representative assemblies. That will be the route briefly pursued here. One function exalted by John Stuart Mill is that of simply *expressing public opinion.*[60] At voicing opinions held by significant numbers of voters back in the constituencies, the United States Congress is extraordinarily effective. There is direct payment for services rendered; the politics of position taking assures that voter sentiments will be echoed.[61] The diversity of the constituencies makes it likely that any given sentiment will find an official voice somewhere. Hence Congress emerges as a cacophonous chorus, its members singing different tunes but always singing something.

One effect of this free-wheeling opinion expression is that criticism of executive conduct is both more versatile and more voluminous than in a typical cabinet regime.[62] There is not the constraint of party

60. Mill, *Considerations on Representative Government*, p. 211.

61. Cf. Bryce on the United States: "There is no country whose representatives are more dependent on popular opinion, more ready to trim their sails to the last breath of it." *The American Commonwealth*, I: 42.

62. The same point is made in K. C. Wheare, *Legislatures* (New York: Oxford University Press, 1963), pp. 142–43.

loyalty to keep majority members from criticizing and
minority members from developing their own individual lines. The idea of an "opposition" achieves idi-
osyncratic realization. In recent decades presidents
have been harassed most resolutely not by official
opposite-party spokesmen (Carl Albert an opposition
leader? Everett Dirksen?), but by congressmen as often
as not of the presidential party with aroused public
followings. On national security policy, where opposition has been most intense, Roosevelt had to contend
with Senator Burton D. Wheeler (D., Mont.), Truman
and Eisenhower with Senator Joseph McCarthy,
Johnson and Nixon with Senator J. William Fulbright. Senator Sam J. Ervin, Jr. (D., N.C.) on
Watergate follows in the tradition of Senator Thomas
J. Walsh (D., Mont.) on Teapot Dome.[63] Often the
voicing of public opinion has policy effects without any
laws being passed; presidents, bureaucrats, and judges,
anticipating trouble with Congress, take action to
avoid it. Thus the congressional uprising during the
Tet offensive of 1968 (no legislation was passed) was a
contributing element in President Johnson's decision
to stop escalating the Vietnam War. As an expressive

63. The congressional reaction to Teapot Dome was generally
more partisan than the reaction to Watergate. Still the Teapot
Dome investigation was sustained for several years by a Senate
with a formal Republican majority. See the account in Burl
Noggle, *Teapot Dome: Oil and Politics in the 1920's* (New York: W. W.
Norton and Co., 1962).

institution Congress, in short, is noisy, versatile, and effective. And it is worth pointing out that the versatility extends over time; public opinion shifts can be registered without changing the membership when politicians have their ears to the ground.

A second function is that of *handling constituent requests.* Sometimes, when the requests have to do with grievances against officialdom, this becomes an "ombudsman" function. Here again there is direct payment for services rendered; the politics of credit claiming gives congressmen a strong incentive to supply particularized benefits and to supply them quickly and efficiently. With their office facilities United States congressmen are probably better equipped than members of any other national parliamentary body to supply these benefits.

The overall policy effects of congressional servicing activities have been given little scholarly attention. Gellhorn is skeptical, his argument being that favors requiring intervention in the bureaucracy bring only episodic constituent relief without changing bureaucratic procedures.[64] Another problem is that there is almost certainly a class bias in servicing activities, a

64. Walter Gellhorn, *When Americans Complain: Governmental Grievance Procedures* (Cambridge: Harvard University Press, 1966), pp. 77–86. If congressional intervention has the sole effect of speeding up redress for one constituent, there is another difficulty: raising one case to the top of the pile and lowering the others may contribute nothing to the sum of human satisfaction. P. 77.

bias that appears by moderately strong inference in data on what kinds of people write letters to their congressmen. A 1965 national survey posing the question "Have you written to your congressman during the last 12 months?" yielded these proportions of affirmative responses: income of $0–4,999, 4.8 percent; $5,000–9,999, 9.1 percent; $10,000–14,999, 19.5 percent; over $15,000, 21.0 percent. And by education: not completed high school, 3.8 percent; completed high school, 13.0 percent; completed college, 25.0 percent. In the occupations, business executives led the field with 19.4 percent; unskilled workers lagged at 4.7 percent.[65] Yet these percentages are high enough to suggest that there are millions of letters annually in each class category. The congressional recourse is there for anyone who is aware of it and wants to use it. It may provide a way of registering need intensity not available through administrative channels. Moreover, in an age of proliferating bureaucracies it would be foolish to derogate any governmental process that offers individual attention. In *Political Ideology* Lane found the following image of congressmen among his working-class interviewees: "From the Congress, and more particularly from the idea of

65. Roper data supplied by the Roper Center. In their elite sample of heads of business organizations, Bauer et al. found that three-fourths of them had communicated with congressmen at one time or another on matters other than foreign-trade policy. *American Business and Public Policy*, p. 201.

home-state congressmen, these men derive a sense of protection, of a friend in power, of an accessible person who is not likely to be protected by a number of secretaries. The right of petition here is expressed in personal, human contact, not through paper forms and proper channels." [66]

For the functions of *legislating* and *overseeing administration* (to be considered together here) the story is at once more interesting and vastly more complicated. As individual responsibility for what Congress passes or what the government does becomes less readily attributable, the relation between payment and services becomes obscured. On the other hand, there do exist opportunities for claiming credit. Analyzing what happens in legislating would be simple enough if measures to be voted on in Congress were prepared and worded by some unspecified outside source, if congressmen did not communicate with each other or the source, and if all approved measures were automatically implemented. In these circumstances Congress would be something like a referendum electorate, and the activities of its members would be distilled into pure position taking. But in these circumstances Congress would not look much like an American

66. Robert E. Lane, *Political Ideology* (New York: Free Press, 1962), p. 148. For an especially good example of a constituent grievance redressed by a senator's intervention and apparently not redressable anywhere else see Douglas, *In the Fullness of Time*, pp. 342–45.

legislative body. There are at least three things congressmen do or can do that violate the referendum principle: (1) They can engage in mobilization activity on pieces of legislation. This may require only nose-counting, in itself an exhausting enterprise in an assembly of 100 or 435. It may also require bargaining—trading away votes on other bills or modifying the legislation at hand to attract support. (2) They determine the content of measures they vote on. Acceptance of presidential formulations is in a sense an alternative here, but acceptance is itself a choice. (3) They can affect the way legislation is implemented by giving postenactment cues to the bureaucracy. Behind the cues lies the threat of future legislation, but in a relation of anticipated responses the cues may be sufficient. The ways in which congressmen do these three things, and in the cases of (1) and (3), the extent to which they do them, are the products of an interplay between credit-claiming and position-taking impulsions.

Vote mobilization in legislative bodies has been the subject of a good deal of theoretical speculation but surprisingly little empirical research. Probably the dominant image is one of "the legislative struggle," of a furious scrambling among members for victories. In one view—Riker's in *The Theory of Political Coalitions*— we should expect politicians in legislative bodies and other settings to form "minimum winning coalitions," the logic being that members of winning majorities

can maximize benefits for their supporters by splitting
the loot as few ways as possible (normally among 51
percent). A possible corollary of this idea is that we
should expect congressional roll calls to be close. The
short empirical response is that most of them are not.
Figure 1 gives frequency distributions of proportions of
House and Senate roll calls won by percentages in
specified ranges in the year 1972. (Whether or not
motions carried is irrelevant here; what is recorded in
each case is the vote percentage won by the winning
side.) No data are included for the many motions
carried without formal roll calls. The distributions for
both houses are bimodal, with a mode in the marginal
range (50–59.9 percent) and a mode in the unanimity
or near-unanimity range (90–100 percent).[67] In both
houses fewer than 30 percent of the roll calls turn up in
the 50–59.9 percent range. It is hard to know what to
make of these marginal modes. They could be evidence that at least on some occasions congressmen try

67. Distributions for some of the state legislatures look about the
same. There are data on Texas in Donald S. Lutz and Richard W.
Murray, "Coalition Formation in the Texas Legislature: Issues,
Payoffs, and Winning Coalition Size," paper presented to the
annual convention of the Midwest Political Science Association,
1972. And there are data on New Jersey, Alabama, Tennessee, and
Wisconsin in David H. Koehler, "Coalition Formation in Selected
State Legislatures," paper presented to the same convention. The
modes at the near-unanimity extreme tend to be higher in these
legislatures than in Congress. New Jersey has no trace of a mode at
the marginal extreme.

to build minimum winning coalitions. But the same modes would appear if there were "natural" position cleavages in the membership or indeed if members were casting their votes randomly.

Although there is a lack of evidence, it makes sense

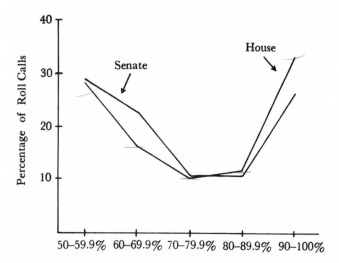

Percentage of Votes Won on a Roll Call by the Winning Side

Figure 1. Frequency Distributions of Proportions of House and Senate Roll Calls Won by Percentages in Specified Ranges, 1972

SOURCE: *Congressional Quarterly Weekly.* Figures are included for all recorded House and Senate roll call votes in the year 1972, except those where the victory requirement was $\frac{2}{3}$ (i.e. treaties, Senate cloture votes, rules suspensions, veto overrides, Constitutional amendments). Senate N = 501. House N = 287. Percentages are of total votes cast on each roll call (rather than of total membership).

at least to try to get the theory straight.[68] On legislation supplying particularized benefits two points may reasonably be made. The first is that it is vital for members to win victories; a dam is no good unless it is authorized and built. The second is that winning victories can be quite easy; the best way for members to handle the particular is to establish inclusive universalistic standards. Thus the House Interior Committee churns out an enormous number of bills, and of the ones that pass the House about 95 percent go through without formal roll calls at all.[69] In other areas the same effect can be achieved by use of "omnibus" bills. Hence on particularized benefits there is no reason to expect to find minimal winning coalitions or close roll calls.

But on legislation bereft of particularized benefits there is another reason not to look for minimal winning coalitions. The members' intrinsic interest in winning vanishes; the bills promise no governmental effects that members can claim personal credit for. Hence the image of members on the winning side

68. A root problem in Riker's formulation is that he begins by declaring the relationship between elected officials and their electorates to be a "fiduciary" relationship. *Theory of Political Coalitions*, pp. 24–28. This gives away the game at the start. In fact the electoral process guarantees not that there will be a fiduciary relationship, but only that politicians will make it *appear* as if there were one. The distinction is critical.

69. Fenno, *Congressmen in Committees*, p. 258.

"splitting up the loot" is inapplicable; there is no politically relevant loot. A good example of legislation devoid of any trace of particularized benefits is the previously mentioned school bussing legislation of the Ninety-second Congress. The Detroit congressmen had every reason to worry about whether they were voting on the right side but no reason to worry about what passed or was implemented. The electoral payment was purely for positions taken. Of course congressmen must at all times generate an impression that they are interested in winning victories, but there may not be much behind the impression. The simple fact that Congress records a roll call, whether close or one-sided, supplies no evidence that anyone has engaged in any mobilizing activity.

When will they mobilize? The short answer is that they will do so when somebody of consequence is watching, when there is credit to be gained for legislative maneuvers. The most alert watchers are doubtless representatives of attentive interest groups— or, more broadly, of attentive clientele groups straddling the public and private sectors. They may be able to detect whether or not a congressman can "deliver." Surprisingly little precise evidence exists on just how programs like the agricultural and merchant marine subsidies win congressional majorities year after year, but the strong likelihood is that relevant congressmen are sufficiently motivated by clientele scrutiny to engage in the bargaining needed to keep them going.[70] To use Lindblom's term, "partisan mutual adjustment" prevails.[71] Of course there are other watchers besides clientele agents. "Good government" outfits such as Common Cause may point out which congressmen are taking the trouble to engage in mobilization. On occasion the audience for maneuvers becomes quite large, as in 1964 when CBS stationed Roger Mudd outside the Capitol for several weeks to give daily television accounts on who was doing what in moving along the civil rights bill on public accommodations.

Yet scrutiny has its limits. Congressional processes are so complicated that it is very difficult for outsiders to tell what is going on. On matters where the audience for congressmen's activities is not a closely scrutinizing one, the incentive to mobilize diminishes. Mobilization, after all, requires time and energy; it may require the trading away of valued goods. Con-

70. Do the agricultural programs offer what have been defined here as "particularized benefits?" Probably not, or not many, although the subject area is murky. A tip-off is that congressmen displayed hardly any interest in what we now call "farm programs" until the Farm Bureau set up shop in Washington in the early 1920s. The formation of the congressional "farm bloc" quickly followed. If farm programs could have been particularized, the congressmen probably would have been peddling benefits long before the 1920s.

71. Lindblom, *The Intelligence of Democracy*, pp. 126–31.

gressmen always have other things to do—such as making speeches, meeting constituents, looking into casework. To put too much into mobilization would be to misallocate resources. For members who make the motions or carry the bills there may be a value in winning, but how much of a value? A congressman can hardly be blamed if there are not enough right-thinking members around to allow him to carry his motions. He's fighting the good fight. On large contentious issues with broad audiences observers realize that most members' positions are fixed anyway.[72] In the Ninety-second Congress Senator Robert P. Griffin (R., Mich.) no doubt found it quite useful to be the ostentatious purveyor of an antibussing amendment, but did it make much difference to him whether it carried? In fact does anybody remember whether it carried? Would Senators Mark O. Hatfield (R., Oreg.) and George McGovern (D., S.D.) have been any the more esteemed by their followers if their antiwar amendment had won rather than lost? Partic-

72. In their study of Texas roll calls Lutz and Murray found that the closest votes were on "moral issues"—prostitution, blue laws, liquor, racetrack betting, etc. "Coalition Formation in the Texas Legislature," pp. 11, 28. These are precisely the kinds of issues on which a model of minimum winning coalitions is least applicable. Every member worries about how he should stand and none about which side wins. If each constituency is homogeneous in its views, every member is in a sense a "winner," regardless of how close or one-sided the roll calls are.

ularized benefits aside, the blunt fact is that congressmen have less of a stake in winning victories than they
normally appear to have.[73]

Indeed, to look at the point another way, we do not
ordinarily think of losses as being politically harmful.
We can all point to a good many instances in which
congressmen seem to have gotten into trouble by being
on the *wrong* side in a roll call vote, but who can think
of one where a member got into trouble by being on
the *losing* side? A decade ago the southern senators
took a last-ditch stand on civil rights; they lost
heroically, but at no time were their jobs in danger.
That the pressure to win is only modest is an
enormously important fact of life in Congress and
doubtless in assemblies generally. If members had to
win all the time, they would tear each other to shreds.

73. Journalists commonly offer better insights on congressional
affairs than social scientists. An example is this comment of
Elizabeth Drew: "The quality of ego that motivates people to seek
political office is not conducive to collective action once they
succeed. Each member of Congress is wont to consider himself a
sort of autonomous principality, sent forth to Washington by an
adulatory constituency. Having arrived, they find it difficult to
accommodate their views, work for legislation that does not bear
their name, or spend time on the dreary business of seeking each
other's support and counting the votes on forthcoming bills. What's
more, the lawmakers come to learn that this is not the sort of thing
to which glory attaches. A thumping speech is more likely to
attract the attention of the press galleries and the hometown
papers than is quiet work in the corridors to change national
policy." Drew, "Members of Congress Are People," *New York
Times*, January 29, 1973, p. 29.

When combined with universalism on particularized benefits, the ability of its members to survive losses renders Congress the most effectively integrative institution in American politics; its members can live in a "cocoon of good feeling."

How much mobilization occurs in Congress is still an empirical question. Probably less than is commonly supposed.[74] Members in both houses seem to offer a lot of floor amendments with nothing accompanying them except speeches. An interview with Senator James L. Buckley (R., N.Y.) shortly after he took office (he was still a political innocent and for that reason a good observer) contained this comment: "He has been surprised, he said, to discover that so many things happen in the Senate 'for symbolic reasons' rather than practical reasons, such as the practice of Senators offering amendments that they know have absolutely no chance of passing." [75] Fenno's account of the

74. Clapp points intriguingly to what may be a barrier in logrolling activity between what goes on in particularized areas and what goes on elsewhere: "Although the legislators are sympathetic to the pleas of colleagues that they support projects that may be expected to benefit the latter in home districts, they react in a much more detached and objective way to the arguments of associates who have come to be recognized as spokesmen for important interest groups. The importance of the local project to electoral success is a matter of which they are quite aware, and a member pleading his own cause receives attention, understanding, and usually cooperation, particularly if he does not request the support of his colleagues often. Congressmen who represent large interests are less successful." *The Congressman*, pp. 181–82.

activities of the House Education and Labor Committee is a classic picture of nonmobilization.[76] An executive official: "When an Education and Labor bill is on the floor, things are so confused that the members don't even know who is in charge of the bill. There are amendments coming out of your ears. . . . From the beginning every bill is accompanied by bickering. Powell, Mrs. (Edith) Green, (Carl) Perkins, and (John) Brademas are all talking at once, vying to see who will get what. And it shakes the confidence of the Members of the House." [77] Fenno: "More often than our other five Committees [in the Fenno study], Education and Labor members will be reluctant to choose 'something' over 'nothing'. More often than the other five, they will prefer a live political issue to a passed compromise bill." [78] The committee's success rate on the House floor is low.[79] It is an interesting question how much mobilizing activity went on in the Senate antiwar campaign of the late 1960s and early 1970s. One constant problem was a kind of product

---

75. Richard L. Madden, "Buckley after 100 Days in Washington: At Ease in Senate Role," *New York Times*, May 2, 1971, p. 20.

76. Of course the labor unions watch the committee closely. But on "causes" beyond labor-management relations the unions themselves commonly play a position-taking role.

77. Fenno, *Congressmen in Committees*, pp. 239–40. The congressmen are the late Adam Clayton Powell (D., N.Y.), Edith Green (D., Oreg.), Carl Perkins (D., Ky.), and John Brademas (D., Ind.).

78. Ibid., p. 234.

79. Ibid., p. 235.

differentiation—senators each coming up with their own peace plans.[80] Over all it may just be true that the level of mobilization activity in Congress is declining. Electoral demand for position taking seems to be on the rise. In the House taciturn machine congressmen are being replaced by voluble city reformers and suburbanites. City and state blocs once maneuverable for logrolling purposes are crumbling.[81] For a member with a reasonably alert middle-class constituency the best course is probably to register an elaborate set of pleasing positions, a course that reduces the chances of vote trading.[82] As an approximation of congressional behavior the referendum model is not quite as far-fetched as it may appear.

What happens in determining the content of measures and in overseeing implementation is also the result of an interplay between credit-claiming and

80. For a provocative commentary see John Rothchild, "Cooing Down the War: The Senate's Lame Doves," *Washington Monthly*, August 1971, pp. 6–19.

81. See "Power in the House: Days of the Brokers Are Gone," *Congressional Quarterly Weekly*, April 7, 1973, pp. 767–71.

82. Thus city machine congressmen have been more willing to vote for farm price support programs (probably as a trade) than city reformers. An infinitely alert public would encourage vote trading in its own interest, but publics are not infinitely alert. At times American reformers have tried to get rid of legislative logrolling. Thus, reports Truman, the Mississippi constitution of 1890 "required legislators to take an oath that they would not trade votes." David B. Truman, *The Governmental Process* (New York: Knopf, 1960), p. 368.

position-taking impulsions. (Of course, content can be shaped by what goes on in mobilization.) The important point here is that on measures lacking particularized benefits the congressmen's intrinsic interest in the impact of legislation vanishes. Hence, it is a misallocation of resources to devote time and energy to prescription or scrutiny of impact unless, again, credit is available for legislative maneuvering. On matters where credit-claiming possibilities wear thin, therefore, we should not be surprised to find that members display only a modest interest in what goes into bills or what their passage accomplishes.[83] Thus Dexter, after interviews in the late 1950s with scores of staff and congressmen on the military committees, concluded that their members had a vigorous interest only in particularistic real estate transactions—"the location of installations and related transfer, purchase, and sale of properties."[84] On other military matters: "How do the members of the relevant committees reach their

83. This point is irrelevant to those economists in the public finance tradition who look only at budgets. (Niskanen is an exception.) Where analysis stops with budgets all governmental expenditures are in principle rather like transfer payments; the impact of spending is irrelevant. Looking at impact becomes important when government is conceived as an agency for making things happen rather than just for cutting up pies. Some of the most significant governmental decisions require no spending at all.

84. Lewis A. Dexter, "Congress and the Making of Military Policy," ch. 8 in Peabody and Polsby, *New Perspectives on the House*, p. 182.

decisions and evaluate the proposals made by the military? The answer seems to be that usually no such evaluation is made." [85] On broad policy the members did, of course, generate what Dexter calls a "rhetoric of justification." [86] On the Senate Foreign Relations Committee, with no real estate transactions to evoke interest, it seems to be difficult to get members to do legislative work at all. For one thing Foreign Relations has a serious attendance problem; in the words of Chairman Fulbright, "This is the kind of committee that Senators like to be on, but they don't like to do anything." [87] On House Education and Labor the concern for programmatic impact is, to say the least, restrained; an executive official's appraisal: "The

85. Ibid., p. 185.

86. Ibid., p. 176. Dexter has these other statements: "Congressmen interviewed generally indicate that they have little tendency to raise or consider questions of military policy *in terms of its meaning for some national or international political objective or goal. . . .* In fact, during the 1946–57 period, few examples could be found where congressional committees created any impression of seriously evaluating decisions about weapons, appropriations, personnel, missions, organization, or administration in terms of national or international goals or objectives." P. 176. For a more recent comment on Congress, the military, and policy impact, see Charles L. Schultze et al., *Setting National Priorities: The 1973 Budget* (Washington, D.C.: Brookings, 1972), pp. 171–74. The conclusion is about the same as Dexter's.

87. John W. Finney, "Study in Absenteeism: One Senate Committee's Week," *New York Times*, January 30, 1972, p. 20. On Foreign Relations see also Fenno, *Congressmen in Committees*, pp. 187–90.

work habits of the members are terrible and it makes
for bad legislation. These habits become the norm.
. . . The younger members of the Committee have a
unique opportunity. They can get amendments in the
bill, amendments galore. They can speak up and
participate all over the place. Nothing about being
seen and not heard on this committee. They can make
speeches knowing that no one will contradict them,
because nobody knows enough. No one knows the
bills." [88] In recent years the House Interior Committee
has attracted a small corps of members dedicated to
the cause of environmentalism rather than to supplying constituency benefits. But they seem to skimp on
their homework. There is this comment by an official
of Friends of the Earth, a preservationist group: "They
are usually preoccupied with their other committee
assignment. So they don't provide any leadership.
They vote with us, but they don't take the time to
learn about the subject matter. They don't have a real
interest." [89] And so it goes. The congressmen's lack of
interest in impact has as a corollary a lack of interest
in "research." To assign committee staffs or the
Congressional Research Service to do research on the

88. Fenno, *Congressmen in Committees*, p. 104.
89. Ibid., p. 286. Fenno adds: "The Committee members who *do*
know the subject matter and *do* take a real interest are those with
goals of constituency service and re-election. Mostly Westerners,
the stakes are, for them, more immediate and the incentives to
participate higher." P. 287.

nonparticularistic effects of legislation (research before or after enactment) would be to misallocate resources. Hence, generally speaking, congressmen do not so assign them. They can find a good many more useful things for staff members and the C.R.S. to do.[90] The conclusions that hold here for enactment of legislation hold also for oversight; in general, members intervene effectively in the bureaucracy on matters where they can claim credit for intervention.[91]

Now, if these are the impulsions behind legislating and overseeing, what are the effects? What seems to happen is that congressional policy-making activities produce a number of specifiable and predictable policy effects. Taken together these effects display what might be called an "assembly coherence"—an overall policy pattern that one might expect any set of

90. Former Senator A. S. Mike Monroney (D., Okla.), a practical reformer of congressional institutions and procedures, voiced this not unusual judgment on the old Legislative Reference Service (now the C.R.S.): "We have great criticism in a wide area of the failure of the Legislative Reference Service to measure up as a reservoir of high research talent that would be available generally to the Congress. I personally have expressed the view in these hearings, and I believe it, that one of the failures is that Congress itself will misuse the Legislative Reference Service for constituent mail, the writing of senior class themes and term papers and doctorate papers and things of that kind, rather than informing Congress on the basic things." Hearings on the Organization of Congress, p. 814.

91. The best theoretical treatment of oversight is in Scher, "Conditions for Legislative Control."

assemblies constructed like the United States Congress
to generate.[92]

One effect is ~~delay~~—or, more properly, since the eye
of the beholder creates it, a widespread perception of
delay. Not too much should be made of this, but it is
fair to say that over the years Congress has often
lagged behind public opinion in enacting major legis-

92. In recent years the study of policy effects has effloresced
among analysts writing in a number of different scholarly tradi-
tions. The range of writings on policies substantially shaped by
Congress includes the following: James T. Bonnen, "The Distribu-
tion of Benefits from Cotton Price Supports," in Samuel B. Chase
(ed.), *Problems in Public Expenditure Analysis* (Washington, D.C.:
Brookings, 1968); on urban renewal: Theodore J. Lowi, *The End of
Liberalism* (New York: W. W. Norton and Co., 1969), ch. 9;
Richard Urban and Richard Mancke, "Federal Regulation of
Whisky Labelling: From the Repeal of Prohibition to the Present,"
15 *Journal of Law and Economics* 411–26 (1972); Richard S. Sterne,
Alvin Rabushka, and Helen A. Scott, "Serving the Elderly—An
Illustration of the Niskanen Effect," 13 *Public Choice* 81–90 (1972);
A. Bruce Johnson, "Federal Aid and Area Redevelopment," 14
Journal of Law and Economics 275–84 (1971); James W. Davis, Jr.,
and Kenneth M. Dolbeare, "Selective Service and Military
Manpower: Induction and Deferment Policies in the 1960's," ch. 5
in Austin Ranney (ed.), *Political Science and Public Policy* (Chicago:
Markham, 1968); Yale Brozen, "The Effect of Statutory Mini-
mum Wage Increases on Teen-Age Employment," 12 *Journal of
Law and Economics* 109–122 (1969); on national policies generally:
Schultze et al., *Setting National Priorities*, ch. 15. There is an analysis
of the attention (or rather the lack of it) that Congress gave to
impact at the time it considered a policy decision in Aaron
Wildavsky, "The Politics of ABM," *Commentary*, November 1969,
pp. 55–63.

lation.[93] Thus a perceived "inaction" was the major source of dissatisfaction with Congress in a survey of a generally dissatisfied public in 1963.[94] Or the delay may exist in the eyes of elites; President Kennedy's tax cut proposal of 1963 and President Johnson's tax increase proposal of 1967, both set forth for the purpose of fiscal management, each took a year to wend its way through a Democratic Congress.[95] Recurrent perceptions of congressional delay on nonparticularized matters should cause little surprise. Mobilization may be halfhearted; there are so many other things to do; some issues may be uncomfortable to vote on at all; a live issue may be better than a live program; the effects are not important anyway.

A second effect is *particularism*—that is, a strong tendency to wrap policies in packages that are salable as particularized benefits. Not only do congressmen aggressively seek out opportunities to supply such

93. Thus, for example, this critique: "The people of this country . . . are, as it seems to me, thoroughly tired of the stagnation of business and the general inaction of Congress. They are disgusted to see year after year go by and great measures affecting the business and political interests of the country accumulate at the doors of Congress and never reach the stage of action." The author was Henry Cabot Lodge in 1889. Quoted in George B. Galloway, *History of the House of Representatives* (New York: Crowell, 1961), p. 133.

94. Davidson et al., *Congress in Crisis*, pp. 56–59.

95. See G. L. Bach, *Making Monetary and Fiscal Policy* (Washington, D.C.: Brookings, 1971), pp. 118, 155.

benefits (little or no "pressure" is needed), they tend in framing laws to give a particularistic cast to matters that do not obviously require it. The only benefits intrinsically worth anything, after all, are ones that can be packaged.[96] Thus in time of recession congressmen reach for "accelerated public works" bills listing projects in the various districts; presidents prefer more general fiscal effects. In the education field a congressional favorite is the "impacted areas" program with its ostentatious grants to targeted school districts; again presidents prefer ventures of more diffuse impact. Presidents are capable of closing a hundred veterans' hospitals like a shot in the interest of "efficiency"; congressmen combine to keep them open. The handling of revenue policy is particularistic; in Manley's exhaustive treatment of congressional tax processes there is hardly any mention of an interest in fiscal effects (though of course the members must worry about how it *looks* to vote for a tax cut or tax increase). Rather the concern is with distributive effects. The highly talented staff of the Joint Commit-

96. The only theories of legislative logrolling that make any sense are the ones that impose information costs on observers. Thus Barry on the "pork barrel": ". . . [I]t is perhaps easy to guess that logrolling under conditions of imperfect information will tend to produce over-investment in projects which yield specific benefits to determinate groups, because such benefits are highly visible to the beneficiaries whereas costs are not so visible to the general taxpayer." *Political Argument*, p. 318.

tee on Internal Revenue Taxation, serving both Senate Finance and House Ways and Means, is in the business of "explicating . . . how individuals and groups will be affected by changes in the Internal Revenue code." [97] Across policy areas generally the programmatic mainstay of congressmen is the categorical grant. In fact the categorical grant is for modern Democratic Congresses what rivers and harbors and the tariff were for pre–New Deal Republican Congresses. It supplies goods in small manipulable packets. "Congressmen . . . like categorical programs because of the opportunities they afford to interfere in administration and thus to secure special treatment, or at least the appearance of it, for constituents among whom . . . state and local as well as federal agencies sometimes figure prominently." [98] The quest for the particular impels congressmen to take a vigorous interest in the organization of the federal bureaucracy. Thus, for example, the Corps of Army Engineers,

97. Manley, *The Politics of Finance*, p. 309. Coleman makes the relevant point that Keynesian macroeconomics is after all an "organic-type theory" not built by aggregating individual preferences. "The fact that Keynes' goal is a benevolent one, supposedly beneficial to the people, has often obscured the fact that its perspective is that of the state, and that there is no microeconomic substructure through which individual pursuit of their interests leads to a Keynesian policy." "Individual Interests and Collective Action," pp. 53–54.

98. Edward C. Banfield, "Revenue Sharing in Theory and Practice," *The Public Interest*, Spring 1971, pp. 41–42.

structured to undertake discrete district projects, must be guarded from presidents who would submerge it in a quest for "planning." [99]

A third effect is the *servicing of the organized*.[100] This takes two familiar forms. First there is a deference toward nationally organized groups with enough widespread local clout to inspire favorable roll call positions on selected issues among a majority of members. Thus under four presidents in a row—Harding through Roosevelt—Congress passed veterans' bonus bills, the presidents vetoed them, and the House voted decisively to override the vetoes.[101] In recent years the

99. On struggles over the corps under Roosevelt and Truman see Maass, *Muddy Waters*, chs. 3, 5. Particularism is no doubt universal. It is hard to top this example drawn from the experience of the Italian parliament of the late nineteenth century: "The deputies, in fact, look upon themselves as agents to procure favors for their constituents, and a striking illustration of the extent to which this is carried is furnished by the difficulty the government found when it managed the railroads in running fast express trains, on account of the interference of the members of the chamber, who insisted that all the trains passing through their districts should stop at way stations." A. L. Lowell, *Governments and Parties in Continental Europe* (Boston: Houghton-Mifflin, 1896), I: 220.

100. Sets of voters who are organized for political action should not be confused with sets of voters who have intense preferences. Whether the latter become the former depends upon whether there are incentives to organize and stay organized. One specific pattern is that producers have better incentives than consumers. On the general point see Mancur Olson, Jr., *The Logic of Collective Action* (Cambridge: Harvard University Press, 1965), pp. 125–31; and Barry, *Political Argument*, p. 273.

101. E. E. Schattschneider, *Party Government* (New York: Rinehart, 1959), p. 194. In the 1930s, 1931 and 1936 were the only

National Rifle Association has weighed in against gun
control legislation.[102] Second, there is deference toward
groups with disposable electoral resources whose representatives keep a close watch on congressional maneuvers. Clientelism at the committee level is the result,
with its manifestations across a wide range of policy
areas. Agriculture is an obvious example.[103] Clientelism, like particularism, gives form to the federal
bureaucracy. Congressmen protect clientele systems—
alliances of agencies, Hill committees, and clienteles—
against the incursions of presidents and cabinet secretaries.[104]

---

years in which the fiscal effects of tax and spending activities of
American governments (at all levels) were clearly countercyclical.
In both cases the Keynesian instruments were apparently veterans'
bonus bills passed over presidential vetoes (Hoover's and Roose-
velt's). See E. Cary Brown, "Fiscal Policies in the Thirties: A
Reappraisal," 46 *American Economic Review* 483 (1956).

102. National polls lean one way on gun control; Congress leans
the other. "It is difficult to imagine any other issue on which
Congress has been less responsive to public sentiment for a longer
period of time." Hazel Erskine, "The Polls: Gun Control," 36
Public Opinion Quarterly 456 (1972).

103. There is an analysis of agricultural clientelism in Lowi, *The
End of Liberalism*, pp. 102–15. A clientele system less developed in
Congress than in some European parliaments is the one in
education. With the nationalization of educational financing it
seems likely that the two congressional houses will sooner or later
create independent education committees (separate from labor)
whose members will service education groups in bipartisan fashion.

104. The best analysis of the impact of congressmen's electoral
needs on the organization of the executive branch is in Harold

A fourth effect is *symbolism.* The term needs explication. It is probably best to say that a purely symbolic congressional act is one expressing an attitude but prescribing no policy effects. An example would be a resolution deploring communism or poverty. But the term *symbolic* can also usefully be applied where Congress prescribes policy effects but does not act (in legislating or overseeing or both) so as to achieve them. No doubt the main cause of prescription-achievement gaps is the intractability of human affairs. But there is a special reason why a legislative body arranged like the United States Congress can be expected to engage in symbolic action by this second, impure construction of the term. The reason, of course, is that in a large class of legislative undertakings the electoral payment is for positions rather than for effects.

An interesting subclass consists of enactments that are "charitable" in nature. That is, they are designed to benefit people other than the ones whose gratification is the payment for passage. If the gratified receive muddled feedback on programmatic accomplishment, the actual supplying of the prescribed benefits becomes a distinctly secondary congressional concern.[105] Thus

Seidman, *Politics, Position, and Power: The Dynamics of Federal Organization* (New York: Oxford University Press, 1970), chs. 2, 5.

105. This argument is taken from Gordon Tullock, "Information without Profit," in Tullock, *Non-Market Decision-Making.* On charitable outfits: "they are 'selling' a feeling of satisfaction derived from sacrifice; whether the sacrifice does or does not

the civil rights acts of 1957 and 1960 were passed to benefit nonvoting southern blacks but to please northern audiences. No one should be surprised that they had little impact in the South.[106] Title I of the Elementary and Secondary Education Act of 1965 allocated money to aid the poor. The audience for the enactment was middle class. In the implementation the money went elsewhere.[107] Laws regulating private conduct have a "charitable" flavor to them. Thus Prohibition—its audience teetotalers and its beneficiaries others who were given the pleasure of having their liquor taken away. That the enforcement was indifferent should cause no surprise.

---

improve the well being of someone else is not of direct interest to the donor. He is interested not in what actually happens, but in his image of it. The entrepreneurs, accordingly, should polish the image." P. 146. The reasoning holds where no financial sacrifice is involved—i.e. where some people write rules governing other people's private behavior.

106. The civil rights acts of 1964 and 1965 did, of course, have considerable impact in the South. For an American legislative venture the 1965 voting rights act was a remarkable exercise in instrumental rationality both in wording and in enforcement. Both these latter acts were substantially presidential creations.

107. See Jerome T. Murphy, "Title I of ESEA: The Politics of Implementing Federal Education Reform," 41 *Harvard Educational Review* 35–63 (1971). "Most federal legislators are sure to be more responsive to the wishes of state and local school officials than to the desires of bureaucrats in the Executive Branch. As a result, the Title I program administrators act as though their main constituency lies in the Congress and the state and local school officials, rather than among the poor whose children the legislation is supposed to assist." P. 51.

In the more general case there is reason to expect
Congress to act "symbolically" whether audiences and
beneficiaries are separate, overlapping, or identical.
Position-taking politics may produce statutes that are
long on goals but short on means to achieve them.[108]
Or bureaucrats may sense that there is little congressional interest in enforcement. Or efforts to achieve
proclaimed goals may run up against congressional
particularism or clientelism. Or all these things may
happen at once. Thus when water pollution became
an issue, it was more or less predictable that Congress
would pass a law characterized as an antipollution act,
that the law would take the form of a grant program
for localities, and that it would not achieve its
proclaimed end.[109] Probably the best examples of
congressional symbolism are those arising out of efforts
to regulate business.[110] Regulatory statutes are the

108. "Within the Congress words are sometimes equated with
deeds. Votes represent final acts. There is a concern with
administration, but it is focused primarily on those elements which
directly affect constituency interests or committee jurisdictions.
Legislative proposals seldom are debated from the viewpoint of
their administrative feasibility." Seidman, *Politics, Position, and
Power*, pp. 65–66.

109. See A. Myrick Freeman and Robert H. Haveman, "Clean
Rhetoric, Dirty Water," *The Public Interest*, Summer 1972, pp.
51–65. The article is only incidentally about Congress, but its
arguments are apposite.

110. Edelman gives prime attention to regulatory policies in his
work on symbolic politics. Murray Edelman, *The Symbolic Uses of
Politics* (Urbana, Ill.: University of Illinois Press, 1967), pp. 23–29.

by-products of congressional position taking at times of
public dissatisfaction. They tend to be vaguely
drawn.[111] What happens in enforcement is largely a
result of congressional credit-claiming activities on
behalf of the regulated; there is every reason to believe
that the regulatory agencies do what Congress wants
them to do.[112] The ambitious "public interest" aims of
the statutes are seldom accomplished.[113] Another place

111. A conclusion of a recent Brookings conference on regulation: "The conference participants generally agreed that the lack
of clarity in regulatory policies creates a critical problem. First, the
Congress has not seen fit to write legislation with specific policy
mandates, preferring fatuous, self-contradictory wish-lists. . . ."
Roger G. Noll, *Reforming Regulation* (Washington, D.C.: Brookings,
1971), p. 101.

112. For a good theoretical treatment of the political economy
of regulation, with statements on the relations between agencies
and Congress, see ibid., pp. 39–46. See also Scher, "Congressional
Committee Members."

113. For a rundown of the literature on the impact of regulation
see Richard E. Caves, "Direct Regulation and Market Performance in the American Economy," 54 *American Economic Review*
172–81 (1964). Two relevant studies giving data on impact of
regulation at the state level are George J. Stigler and Claire
Friedland, "What Can Regulators Regulate? The Case of Electric-
ity," 5 *Journal of Law and Economics* 1–16 (1962); and William A.
Jordan, "Producer Protection, Prior Market Structure and the
Effects of Government Regulation," 15 *Journal of Law and Economics*
151–76 (1972). Stigler and Friedland lean to the conclusion that
regulation has no effect; Jordan, to the conclusion that having it
benefits producers. At the national level the effects of regulatory
acts passed in the 1960s are still unclear. Measured by its
proclaimed goals the Wholesome Meat Act of 1967 is apparently a

where symbolism occurs is in housing programs; there exists no close analysis of housing politics in Congress, but it is fair to say that the programs offer members a complex mix of opportunities for position taking and credit claiming. To point to congressional symbolism is not, of course, to denounce it. The Constitution does not require, nor does political theory decisively insist, that legislative processes enshrine high standards of instrumental rationality. By some defensible criteria it is perfectly proper to put laws on the books and then not to enforce them. Among other things doing so may offer a murky way of maximizing governmental satisfaction of popular preferences; Prohibition is a case in point.[114]

A special word may be in order here on the politics of transfer programs—that is programs giving governmental cash payments to individuals in defined subclasses of the population.[115] What distinguishes American transfer programs is not that they are "redistributive" [116]—they are not any more so than some other

---

disaster. See Simon Lazarus and Leonard Ross, "Rating Nader," *New York Review of Books,* June 28, 1973, p. 32.

114. The state of Mississippi once had a Prohibition law, widespread bootlegging, and at the same time a liquor tax. Would any other arrangement have been as good? See Key, *Southern Politics,* p. 233.

115. For a general treatment of social security see Colin D. Campbell, "Social Insurance in the United States: A Program in Search of an Explanation," 12 *Journal of Law and Economics* 249–65, (1969).

116. Lowi's categorization in "American Business," p. 691.

programs—but that they offer legislators no particularized benefits. Who gets a check of what size is clearly prescribed by law, so congressmen get no credit for the handing out of individual checks. In these circumstances what can be said about the politics? A first point is that Congress will favor the passage of transfer programs when they are championed by powerful interest groups against unorganized opposition; the obvious example is the veterans' bonus. A second point is that Congress will legislate incremental payment increases in existent programs where there is little organized sentiment for or against doing so. Hence the biennial hike in social security benefits. The public assistance program has been enriched in an absentminded way over the years, mostly through the medium of Senate floor amendments.[117] A third point is that Congress will be reluctant to legislate new programs benefiting the unorganized over the opposition of the organized. The third point is important. For members deciding how to vote there is a lack of prospective performance credit to counterbalance the influence of organized opposition. Hence major transfer innovations are unlikely to spring from individualistic assemblies. The impetus comes from elsewhere— Bismarck introduced his innovations for regime reasons; Lloyd George, for party reasons; Roosevelt

117. See Gilbert Y. Steiner, *Social Insecurity: The Politics of Welfare* (Chicago: Rand McNally, 1966), pp. 48–51.

(social security), Johnson (medicare), and Nixon (family assistance), for presidential reasons. A fourth and last point is that the politics of transfers would be vastly different if congressmen were allowed to put their names on the checks.

One final argument on Congress and the legislative function has a different cast to it. The argument is that Congress in a peculiar way is an extraordinarily democratic body. If, on matters beyond the particular, congressmen are judged by positions rather than effects, then what kinds of laws are they likely to write? The answer is that they are much inclined to incorporate popular conceptions of instrumental rationality into the statute books. Attentive publics judge positions on means as well as on ends. Hence the congressional penchant for the blunt, simple action— the national debt limit, the minimum wage,[118] the price rollback, the 10 percent across-the-board budget slash, the amendment cutting off aid to Communist countries, the amendment ending the Vietnam War in ninety days.[119] A good example of an issue where

118. Politically attractive but economically dubious. One analysis in a fairly large literature is Brozen, "The Effect of Statutory Minimum Wage Increases on Teen-Age Employment."

119. A useful way to get a feel for an institution is to examine its language. The *Congressional Record* is full of mares' nests, entering wedges, camels' noses, cans of worms, Pandora's boxes, golden eggs, roosting chickens, pigs in a poke, forests and trees, babies and bathwater. This is the language of common sense, of folk wisdom. It infuses congressional activities. See the fascinating analysis in

popular conceptions prevail is crime; one side tries to bring back the lash or silence the Supreme Court, the other side (with a taste of sociology) goes after the "real causes." [120] If it is widely believed that spending money will "solve social problems," then Congress will spend money. Keynesian economics receives a chillier reception on the Hill than in the White House, not because Congress is more "conservative," but because it is in one sense more democratic; the image of a balanced family budget is a powerful one.[121] The fact that Congress echoes public reasoning makes it necessary that large governmental ventures requiring Capitol Hill approval be explained in advance. Prime Minister Heath could take Britain into the Common Market abruptly, telling the public, in effect, to judge him by the consequences afterward. President Truman had to justify NATO and the Marshall Plan before they were launched. A failure to make persuasive explanations probably underlay the defeat of President Nixon's family assistance plan.[122] The ability of mass publics to prescribe means as well as ends is a

---

Arlen J. Large, "Pandora Opens a Can of Worms," *Wall Street Journal*, August 28, 1973, p. 10.

120. Neither course seems to make much sense. See James Q. Wilson, "If Every Criminal Knew He Would Be Punished If Caught . . . ," *New York Times Magazine*, January 28, 1973, p. 56.

121. Ways and Means Chairman Wilbur Mills (D., Ark.) was still speaking of a balanced federal budget as a desirable norm in its own right in 1969. Bach, *Making Monetary and Fiscal Policy*, p. 155.

122. The plan made it through the House but was sandbagged in the Senate Finance Committee. Daniel P. Moynihan, the

neglected subject of democratic theory. If, as Morton White argues, the question of whether ordinary citizens are capable of making normative appraisals is a central one in democratic theory,[123] so also is the question of whether we are capable of making cognitive appraisals. An institution like the United States Congress can stay afloat only if the public grasp of means-ends relationships is reasonably sophisticated. It does stay afloat, although there are shoals now and then. Probably half the adverse criticism of Congress by elites is an indirect criticism of the public itself. Over time the effectiveness of Congress as a decision-making body can be expected to vary with public sophistication but also with the inherent complexity of governmental affairs.

author of family assistance, says that another committee might have acted differently—perhaps constructively revised the House bill. "But the Senate Finance Committee was not bent to any such norm of prosaic, workmanlike persistence. The senators were individualists, and more than a normal quota were exhibitionists as well. At the expressive, symbolic level of politics they are hardly to be faulted, but there was lacking an eventual seriousness which is the hallmark of mature government." Moynihan, *The Politics of a Guaranteed Income* (New York: Random House, 1973), p. 482. Yes indeed. But the senators, after all, were worried about how the program looked rather than about what was in it. The symbolism was confusing; it was hard to know what position to take.

123. Morton White, *Science and Sentiment in America* (New York: Oxford University Press, 1972).

The mention of staying afloat can serve as a lead-in to a discussion of a different topic. How indeed does Congress stay afloat? The problem is a real one, important enough to require a theoretical modification to deal with it. Consider "assembly coherence" as a set of institutional perils—delay, particularism, servicing of the organized, symbolism. It is easy to conjure up visions of exasperated publics in search of unattainable effects shunting Congress aside and taking their business elsewhere. Efficient pursuit of electoral goals by members gives no guarantee of institutional survival. Quite the contrary. It is not too much to say that if all members did nothing but pursue their electoral goals, Congress would decay or collapse. Some of the institutional maintenance problems are implicit in the earlier discussion, including a serious one arising from the difficulty of getting members to do grueling and unrewarding legislative work.[124] (Sometimes in the Senate it is even hard to get them to appear and vote.)[125]

124. See the section in Clapp, *The Congressman*, entitled "Does Legislative Work Pay Off?" pp. 108–10. The popular image of an effective congressman is probably one of somebody doing a lot of moving and shaking in public. In the classic 1939 film, "Mr. Smith Goes to Washington," the hero, Jefferson Smith (Jimmy Stewart) chose as his mission the building of a boys' camp along Willet Creek. But the sinister Boss Taylor (Edward Arnold) wanted to build a dam in the same place. So what Smith did was to filibuster until he dropped from exhaustion.

125. Senate Majority Leader Mike Mansfield (D., Mont.): "How we can work in a situation like this I don't know. But I am

At least three distinct kinds of maintenance problems can arise in the handling of money, a basic congressional prerogative the exercise of which is central to member electoral quests. The first has to do with allocation. Given popular preferences, will members spend money on various matters at "optimal" levels? Will they distribute tax burdens "fairly"? There may be a predictable tendency to "underspend" in some areas—such as transfers. It is easy to see how particularism and clientelism could produce "distortions" in both taxing and spending. The old image of Congress as a pork barrel outfit can be looked upon as an institutional maintenance problem.[126] The second

at the end of my wits. I do not know any way to keep them here, unless perhaps the local newspapers start publicizing the absenteeism of their Senators." John W. Finney, "Senate's Inaction Exasperates Leaders," *New York Times*, February 7, 1972, p. 25.

126. There is a theoretical economics literature on whether democratic governments can be expected to spend on various matters at optimal levels—i.e. levels geared to popular preferences. Authors differ in their assumptions about information costs and about governmental structure. A recent guide to the literature is J. Ronnie Davis and Charles W. Meyer, "Budget Size in a Democracy," ch. 19 in James M. Buchanan and Robert D. Tollison (eds.), *Theory of Public Choice* (Ann Arbor: University of Michigan Press, 1972). Buchanan and Tullock argue that a government centered in a majority-rule assembly will overspend because of logrolling. *The Calculus of Consent*, chs. 10–12. But the problem of information costs is ignored. Niskanen allows for information costs (e.g. no one is quite sure what the activities of bureaus accomplish) and argues that, if certain assumptions about public opinion distributions are made, a government with close relations between

problem that arises in the handling of money by Congress has to do with overall economic effects. There are the effects of congressional taxing and spending decisions on price and employment levels, and the effects of congressional tariff decisions on price

bureaus and supportive assembly committees will overspend in the areas of those close relations. *Bureaucracy and Representative Government*, ch. 14. What happens, in effect, is that particularism or clientelism or both lead to overspending. Downs argues that a democratic government (structure unspecified) will systematically underspend because of voter information costs. To voters it is clearer where the money comes from (taxes) than where it goes to (programs with diffuse effects). Hence underspending. Anthony Downs, "Why the Government Budget Is Too Small in a Democracy," 12 *World Politics* 541–63 (1960). A possible corollary of the Downs argument is that a government centered in an individualistic assembly will spend less than one organized like, say, the British—the reason being that a government like the British can jam through ill-understood programs and get paid for their effects four or five years later. These authors raise important questions, but there are no certain answers. One problem is the virtual nonexistence of empirical analysis—either of the sort that matches public opinion readings with spending levels or of the sort that compares spending levels in systems with different governmental arrangements. A theoretical problem in allocation thinking is that government budgeting differs from family budgeting in one important respect—on many salient matters no one can be sure what the effects of spending would be. Arguments about cutting up the pie quickly turn into arguments about the effects of giving out slices. Whole ideologies can be spun out on such questions as whether spending can reduce poverty. (Downs discusses the problem of uncertain effects. P. 554.) On the United States Congress it may be that both Niskanen and Downs are right. That is, there may be underspending in some areas for the Downs reason

levels and trade flow. (Whether the tariff should be taken up under money policy is of course unclear; the tariff is a tax, but the direct benefits it confers do not come out of the Treasury.) The institutional danger arises from the fact that congressmen have little or no electoral reason to worry about any of these effects. Yet an institution that generates them blindly is an institution in trouble.[127] The third kind of problem is fiscal in nature, but in a way it is more fundamental. Spending is generally popular and taxes are not. In the public mind the connection between the two is there, but it is decidedly ambiguous.[128] If congressmen reflect public opinion, what is to prevent them from

---

and overspending in others for the Niskanen reason (although it is not clear that bureau empire-building has to enter the picture for particularism or interest-group pressure to induce overspending). This was more or less Woodrow Wilson's conclusion. *Congressional Government*, ch. 3.

127. It is surprisingly difficult to figure out what independent impact congressional money decisions have on price and employment levels. Analytic problems arise because some spending authority is discretionary and some extends over periods of years. Pechman concluded in 1971 that the net effect of congressional decisions had probably been fiscally too restrictive in the preceding decades. Joseph A. Pechman, *Federal Tax Policy* (Washington, D.C.: Brookings, 1971), p. 47. It may be that the piling up of categorical grant programs in the 1960s has tipped the congressional balance to the inflationary side. But this is just a guess. Transfer payments have risen too.

128. See Angus Campbell et al., *The American Voter* (New York: Wiley, 1960), pp. 195–97.

systematically voting in favor of spending but against taxes?[129] Alert public opinion can no doubt act as check on behavior of this sort, but how much of a check? There is a primal danger here that any taxing and spending body has to come to grips with.

One way to stay afloat is to hire people to man the helm. This in effect is what congressmen do. It seems proper here to discuss institutional maintenance as a collective goods problem, following Mancur Olson's arguments in *The Logic of Collective Action*. The case goes as follows: If members hope to spend careers in Congress, they have a stake in maintaining its prestige as an institution. They also have a stake in maintaining congressional control over resources that are useful in electoral quests. But if every member pursues only his own electoral goals, the prestige and power of Congress will drain away. What can be done? The inclination to do anything at all is, of course, minimal; Congress is more fragile than it looks.[130] Yet from the

129. Senator Douglas writes: "One of my closest associates never voted against any appropriation for any purpose, no matter how extravagant or foolish it was. This never hurt him politically. In fact, I think it helped him." *In the Fullness of Time*, p. 312.

130. Fenno, drawing on his recent travels with incumbent House members in their districts, gives this report on what they say to their constituents: "Every Representative with whom I traveled criticized the Congress and portrayed himself, by contrast, as a fighter against its manifest evils. Members run *for* Congress by running *against* Congress." Richard F. Fenno, Jr., "If, as Ralph Nader says, 'Congress is the Broken Branch,' How Come We Love

member point of view the maintenance of the institution is a collective good of some importance.[131] What is needed is a system of "selective incentives"[132] to induce at least some members to work toward keeping the institution in good repair. And it is just such a system that has evolved over the decades. What happens is that prestige and power within the Congress itself are accorded to upholders of the institution; the Capitol Hill pecking order is geared to the needs of institutional maintenance. Members are paid in internal currency for engaging in institutionally protective activities that are beyond or even against their own electoral interests.[133]

Our Congressmen So Much?", manuscript prepared for the *Time* "Role of Congress" series, p. 2.

131. It would not be so important if members did not plan to spend careers there. Therefore, a persuasive argument against reform efforts to limit members to a few years in office is that institutional maintenance would suffer. An analogous argument holds in universities, where permanent faculty have an institutional stake lacking among students and junior faculty. Or at least so it is said.

132. Mancur Olson's term. *The Logic of Collective Action*, p. 51.

133. It may occur to the reader that the earlier discussion of policy making could have been set up as a collective goods problem. That is, on matters like regulatory policy members could have been portrayed as seekers of effects unable to achieve them because of the difficulty of generating collective action. But to argue this way would have been a mistake. The notion of members as seekers of effects needs a razor taken to it; the electoral payment is for positions, not effects. A related point is that the selective incentives discussed above work quite clearly in the interest of

To some extent the incentives apply generally across the membership. Thus the hero of the Hill is not the hero of the airwaves. The member who earns prestige among his peers is the lonely gnome who passes up news conferences, cocktail parties, sometimes even marriage in order to devote his time to legislative "homework." But the most interesting paid protectors are those in official positions—elected leaders in both houses and members of the three "control committees" in the House.[134] Party leaders may not amount to much as partisans, but they are vitally important as institutional protectors. As Fenno says of the more successful House majority leaders and Speakers, "They have been men whose devotion to the House was considered greater than any devotion to ideological causes." [135] Keeping legislative business moving is a major service in itself. But leaders are also on the alert for member activities that threaten to earn Congress a bad reputation. Thus Democratic House leaders put a damper on the House Un-American Activities Committee in the Eighty-first Congress after the HUAC

institutional maintenance and not in the interest of general programmatic performance.

134. Institutional maintenance in the Senate is less tied to formal position. For years the chief "Senate man" was Richard Russell (D., Ga.).

135. Richard F. Fenno, Jr., "The Internal Distribution of Influence: The House," in Truman (ed.), *The Congress and America's Future*, p. 63.

circus in the Eightieth.[136] Speaker Sam Rayburn (D., Tex.) placed a general ban on the televising of House hearings.[137] Leaders have an eye for the more ostentatious ventures in interest-group servicing and particularism. Control of the agenda allows them to bring up matters like veterans' bills on rules suspension motions, requiring a two-thirds vote.[138] They know the dangers of the tariff; Bauer, Dexter, and Pool give an account of Rayburn pleading with House members not to open up an Eisenhower trade bill to floor amendments.[139]

136. See Goodman, *The Committee*, p. 273. At no time since 1938 has a majority of House members been willing to take a position against the committee. But there has been intense opposition to the committee in sections of the public in a position to cast general doubt on Congress's reputation.

137. A Rayburn biographer quotes the late Speaker: " 'When a man has to run for re-election every two years,' he explained, 'the temptation to make headlines is strong enough without giving him a chance to become an actor on television. The normal processes toward good law are not even dramatic, let alone sensational enough to be aired across the land.' " Booth Mooney, *Mr. Speaker* (Chicago: Follett, 1964), p. 167.

138. See Neil MacNeil, *Forge of Democracy: The House of Representatives* (New York: David McKay, 1964), p. 342.

139. Bauer et al., *American Business and Public Policy*, p. 64. Rayburn's attitude has been handed down to his successors. Thus this statement by the new House majority leader, Thomas P. O'Neill (D., Mass.): " 'The country's becoming more protectionist again,' he said. 'You get a tariff on the floor today with an open rule, and there will be 4,000 amendments to it. There are going to be people who want to protect the shoe industry, protect the glass industry, protect the fish industry.' " Marjorie Hunter, "O'Neill of the House: A Majority Leader's Perspective," *New York Times*, January 20, 1973, p. 21.

Some of the major achievements of the Texas leaders can be interpreted as acts of institutional maintenance—Johnson's maneuvering in 1954 to bring about the McCarthy censure, Johnson's maneuvering in 1957 to pass a civil rights bill (symbolic or not, it proved that Congress could pass one),[140] Rayburn's maneuvering in 1961 to pack a Rules Committee holding up bills favored by public opinion.[141]

The three "control committees" of the House—Rules, Appropriations, and Ways and Means—are delicately arranged to contribute to institutional maintenance. (In this respect none of the three has a functional analogue in the Senate.) The inducements to serve on them are the power and prestige within the House that go with membership.[142] Appointments are not easy to get; for several decades congressmen have more eagerly sought places on these committees than

140. For accounts of the 1954 and 1957 maneuverings see Rowland B. Evans and Robert Novak, *Lyndon B. Johnson: The Exercise of Power* (New York: New American Library, 1964), pp. 81–85, 119–40.

141. See Milton C. Cummings, Jr., and Robert L. Peabody, "The Decision to Enlarge the Committee on Rules: An Analysis of the 1961 Vote," ch. 11 in Peabody and Polsby, *New Perspectives on the House.*

142. For Appropriations and Ways and Means there is direct interview evidence that congressmen seek membership because of the power and prestige it offers. See Fenno, *Power of the Purse*, p. 82; Manley, *The Politics of Finance*, p. 56; Fenno, *Congressmen in Committees*, pp. 2–5.

on any others.[143] Appointments on the three go to "responsible" legislators, with this definition of the term: "According to the party leaders and the members of the committees-on-committees, a responsible legislator is one whose ability, attitudes, and relationships with his colleagues serve to enhance the prestige and importance of the House of Representatives." [144] Membership on any of the three is not an electoral liability, and in the case of Appropriations or Ways and Means it can be a considerable asset. But what makes the committees interesting is the set of services each supplies to congressmen as individuals and to the Congress as an institution. In one role each committee gives direct services; it makes decisions that are helpful to individual congressmen in their electoral quests. In another role each committee supplies indirect services; it does things helpful to the Congress as an institution that go beyond or against member electoral quests. This may seem an odd mix, but there is institutional wisdom in it; the committees have to offer the right combination of power and prestige to induce talented members to serve on them.

The Rules Committee's services derive from its power to hold up or expedite bills. It can aid members

143. For the 1914–41 period there are data collected by John C. Eberhart and reported in George B. Galloway, *Congress at the Crossroads* (New York: Crowell, 1946), p. 90.

144. Nicholas A. Masters, "Committee Assignments," ch. 10 in Peabody and Polsby, *New Perspectives on the House*, p. 240.

directly by moving along bills they want or by blocking bills they find it uncomfortable to vote on at all.[145] The best recent example of this latter role is probably the committee's blocking action on federal aid to education in 1961. From the member standpoint the Kennedy education bill was a nightmare; there were crosscutting public opinion cleavages on race, on religion, and on the issue of federal spending. Rules voted 8 to 7 to kill the bill, with James J. Delaney (D., N.Y.) casting the deciding vote. In the liberal press Delaney was a villain, but in the House he was a hero. *Newsweek* reported: " 'When Delaney cast his vote,' one Southerner said, 'you could hear the sigh of relief all over the Capitol.' And hours later in the Speaker's Lobby, grateful congressmen still were shaking the New Yorker's hand." [146] Out of such actions is prestige woven. But Rules also supplies indirect services. With the party leaders it arranges the House agenda.[147] In blocking bills it probably serves as a check on particu-

145. ". . . [A]n institution that dispenses and obscures responsibility has distinct advantages for many of its members, who find it useful to reduce political pressures upon themselves by shifting to others the blame for the success or failure of certain measures. That the House Committee on Rules performs this valuable function is clearly demonstrated by our survey data [a sample of House members showing that a majority were against stripping Rules of its blocking powers]." Davidson et al., *Congress in Crisis*, pp. 104–05.

146. *Newsweek*, July 31, 1961, p. 25.

147. For an account see James A. Robinson, *The House Rules Committee* (Indianapolis: Bobbs-Merrill, 1963), chs. 2, 3.

larism and interest-group servicing; Robinson reports
that the standing committees most often denied rules
for their bills seem to be Veterans' Affairs, Public
Works, and Interior.[148] And it may also serve as a
check on symbolism by blocking proposals that are
unworkable.[149]

The House Appropriations Committee directly aids
congressmen by supplying money for their pet projects.
But its indirect service is far more important. Appropriations acts as the "guardian of the federal Treasury." [150] Its members adopt as their mission the cutting
of budget estimates,[151] and they work remarkably hard
at it.[152] They "cut," "carve," "slice," "prune," "trim,"
"chop," "slash," "shave," and "whack." [153] There is a
custom of arranging subcommittees so that members
do not handle programs they have a direct interest in
financing.[154] The Senate Appropriations Committee

148. Ibid., p. 28.

149. The Rules Committee flashes across the headlines, of
course, at those times when a majority position on important issues
among House members is only a minority position among Rules
members. This happened in the Eighty-first and Eighty-sixth
Congresses, in each case as a result of large gains in Democratic
seat holdings. On these occasions Rules was more conservative
than the House, and there arose the problem of stopping it from
blocking bills favored by a House majority.

150. Fenno, *Power of the Purse*, pp. 98–102.

151. Ibid., pp. 102–08.

152. Ibid., pp. 90–95.

153. Ibid., p. 105.

154. Ibid., p. 149.

has no budget-cutting ethic; it acts as an "appeals court" for agencies that want more money.[155] House committee members disdain senators for their extravagance.[156] All this is well known from Fenno's account. But how do we explain the House committee's activities? In at least four ways the members fill an institutional maintenance role. By cutting budgets they work against the diffuse and primal danger that Congress will spend more money than it takes in. They lean against particularism and also against servicing of the organized. And they lean against symbolism, which the members call "waste"—a term that has disappeared in modern theories of public finance. "Waste" can occur when a standing committee authorizes a billion dollars in a good cause but takes no interest in what happens to the money thereafter; the ostentatious authorization is what counts. To guide them in their manifold efforts Appropriations members recall what is taken to be a past institutional record of sin and redemption. Between 1885 and 1921 most of the appropriations bills were syndicated out among House standing committees, with committees supportive of programs doing both the authorizing and the appropriating. There is a scholarly consensus that this arrangement produced extravagant spending in

155. Ibid., pp. 534–39. The Senate had the same "appeals court" role a century ago. See Wilson, *Congressional Government*, pp. 113–14.

156. Fenno, *Power of the Purse*, pp. 626–32.

the areas of syndication;[157] certainly Appropriations members believe that it did.[158] Redemption came in 1921 with the gathering back of all the appropriations bills into one place. The modern Appropriations Committee enjoys solid House support. Members may get hurt by its decisions now and then, but in general they honor it for its penny-pinching.

House Ways and Means, like Appropriations, serves members directly—in this case mostly by processing special tax provisions. (The Democratic delegation also handles appointments to the other standing committees.) But again the indirect services are more important. In effect Ways and Means is hired to put a damper on particularism in tax and tariff matters and to protect what members call the "actuarial sound-

157. "Such a disintegration of fiscal control was fatal to balancing income and outgo." Leonard D. White, *The Republican Era: 1869–1901* (New York: Macmillan, 1958), p. 65. "With many of the department heads and bureau chiefs sharing in the general irresponsibility of this spending heyday, the rapid growth of federal expenditure during the next decade became a national scandal. The congressional floodgates were open, and funds flowed out unabated for such projects as improvements for rivers and harbors that carried little traffic, and superfluous post offices for tiny villages." Joseph P. Harris, *Congressional Control of Administration* (Washington, D.C.: Brookings, 1969), p. 54. See also Louis Fisher, *President and Congress: Power and Policy* (New York: Free Press, 1972), pp. 92–94.

158. Chairman George Mahon (D., Tex.) makes the case in a speech celebrating the 100th anniversary of the committee. *Congressional Record* (daily ed.), March 2, 1965, pp. 3863–67.

ness" of the social security program.[159] The Senate, where the Finance Committee assumes no such role, tends to differ from the House by voting for lower taxes,[160] higher tariffs,[161] and more liberal transfer benefits.[162] The current Senate instrument is the "Christmas tree bill," laden with goodies of all sorts often added on by floor amendment.[163] Given their mission, Ways and Means members consider it vitally important that the House membership not unravel their bills. The first "strategic premise" of the committee, in Fenno's formulation, is "to write a bill that will pass the House." [164] Accordingly the committee has nurtured the custom of using the "closed rule"—outlawing floor amendments—on tax, tariff, and transfer bills.[165] "The closed rule acts as a shield for Ways and Means bills against hundreds of interest group demands that would be articulated if not fulfilled if the bill appeared naked on the floor." [166] Ways and

159. On social security see Manley, *The Politics of Finance*, p. 281. On the rest, Manley, ch. 6 generally.

160. Ibid., pp. 272–79.

161. Ibid., pp. 281–91.

162. Ibid., pp. 279–81.

163. Ibid., p. 258. "To [Ways and Means] Committee members, the Senate is characterized by irresponsible logrolling and by capitulation to politically popular but unwarranted demands; by the kind of decision-making, in short, that one could expect in the House without the closed rule." P. 250.

164. Fenno, *Congressmen in Committees*, p. 55.

165. Manley, *The Politics of Finance*, p. 226.

166. Ibid., p. 223.

Means, like Appropriations, may deprive congressmen of immediate gratification now and then, but its members are exalted for their institutional service.

It would be absurd, of course, to claim that the institutional maintenance efforts of the leaders and the control committees offer a cure-all for congressional problems. No one exercises much of a check on symbolism; the Appropriations members bring to their search for "waste" a narrow accounting mentality. And to dampen is not to extinguish; the Ways and Means Committee does after all deal in tax loopholes, and it is difficult to get on the committee at all without displaying support for the oil depletion allowance.[167] There is the possibility that congressmen "underspend" in areas where they are not inspired by particularism or organized pressure.[168] And Congress

167. Ibid., pp. 26–27.
168. The liberals tend to think so. That Congress might do so is deducible from the arguments in Downs, "Why the Budget Is Too Small." (See the explication in footnote 126.) What "underspending" means is of course problematic. The public finance theorists build models that aggregate popular preferences. A Rawls definition of "underspending" would be different. See Rawls, *A Theory of Justice.* The dialogue between congressional liberals and conservatives on spending often takes a form in which the arguments of both sides may simultaneously be correct. Liberals insist that the government underspends on causes dear to unorganized constituencies. Conservatives insist that to spend money on such causes is to "waste" it. Give "waste" the connotation of "symbolism," and the conservatives have a point. Certainly most liberal programs advertised as "redistributive" have little or no redistributive effect

has no clear way of generating intended fiscal effects; the effort to set up a joint budgetary committee in the late 1940s foundered in disarray. The fiscal problem surfaced in the winter of 1972–73 as an "impoundment crisis," with President Nixon lashing out at Congress for its alleged inflationary proclivities.[169] It was difficult to tell whether the money conflict between president and Congress was likely to be temporary (i.e. caused by an epiphenomenal difference in supporting coalitions between president and Congress), or chronic (i.e. caused by a shift in congressional programs and processes giving Capitol Hill activities an inflationary bias). The congressional response to impoundment was once again to try to establish a joint budgetary process.[170] Whether it would work was problematic; again there was a collective goods problem.

If the existent institutional maintenance arrange-

---

in practice. See Peter Passell and Leonard Ross, *The Retreat from Riches: Affluence and Its Enemies* (New York: Viking, 1971), ch. 2.

169. A weary reflection on congressional spending programs by Senate Minority Leader Hugh Scott (R., Pa.): "It is difficult because, as I said yesterday, we are all responsible. We voted for these things last year, and some of us will vote for them again. When they come before us after a veto, and the veto is not sustained, we go through the debt ceiling by our own legislation, and we contribute to inflation, which we collectively deplore. Then we face a congressional tax increase, which we always call 'tax reform.' " *Congressional Record* (daily ed.), February 21, 1973, p. S2945.

170. See "Congress and the Budget: Better Days Ahead," *Congressional Quarterly Weekly*, April 28, 1973, pp. 1013–18.

ments in Congress are imperfect, they nonetheless exist. They help to ward off what the past has shown to be real dangers. They are blunt and negative—the three control committees are like governors on what can all too easily become a runaway engine. Within their limits the arrangements are effective. It is hard to see how Congress could maintain its prestige and power without them. And there is an important constitutional point here. To check the modern presidency the Congress after all has to maintain its prestige and power. Hence it is always important that congressional "reformers" go about their task with eyes open; to get rid of the closed rule in the interest of "democratization," for example, would be indirectly to weaken the Congress and strengthen the presidency.[171]

Surely it is easy enough for assemblies to wane or collapse. In the United States, with its flexible constitutional arrangements, decision powers can be transferred to other governmental organs. The history of American city reform is largely a history of taking

171. Of course to give in to selective presidential impoundment would also be to lose power. Congressman Jamie Whitten (D., Miss.) makes this case: "What we must not do is turn over to the executive branch the right to select projects and programs to go forward and those to be killed. If we do that there is no further need for the Congress, for the Congress will have given up the place as the people's branch whose prime responsibility is to look after the people." *Congressional Record* (daily ed.), October 10, 1972, p. H9375.

powers away from city councils. One problem has been council particularism; in Peoria reform meant among other things taking down stop signs the aldermen had put at almost all the city crossroads.[172] There was a time, to be sure, when "bosses" were informally hired to govern; in Chicago the party boss in the mayor's office still serves as a deus ex machina check on council particularism.[173] But over the long haul formal institutional changes have been the pattern— at-large elections to make councilors serve "the city as a whole" rather than their wards, item vetoes to give mayors control over projects, rules outlawing council increases in budget estimates, laws generally strengthening the mayoral office.[174] City councils as a result are burned-out volcanoes here and there disfiguring the urban landscape. The Boston council, write Banfield and Wilson, "has no real function in city government." [175] American councilors do some ombudsman work; they champion the civil service un-

172. John Bartlow Martin, "The Town That Tried Good Government," in Edward C. Banfield (ed.), *Urban Government: A Reader in Politics and Administration* (Glencoe, Ill.: Free Press, 1961), p. 280.

173. Banfield, *Political Influence*, chs. 11, 12.

174. On the logic of city reform see Samuel P. Hays, "Political Parties and the Community-Society Continuum," ch. 6 in Chambers and Burnham, *The American Party Systems*, p. 170; and Edward C. Banfield and James Q. Wilson, *City Politics* (Cambridge: Harvard University Press, 1963), pp. 89–96, ch. 11.

175. Banfield and Wilson, *City Politics*, p. 95.

ions; they fire occasional symbolic broadsides; but worrying about the general impact of government is left to the mayors.

Is it possible for an individualistic assembly to govern all by itself? The United States, with its constitutional mixtures at all levels of government, offers no clear test. But the case of France is illuminating. France, the other great nineteenth-century republic, has had the same problem as the United States in deciding where to locate executive power. The French solution in the Third and Fourth republics, following the logic of the 1790s, was to concentrate power in a set of national assemblies (with the lower house dominant). But France, like the United States, never developed into a party regime. For a brief moment after World War II there were signs that it would, but the alliance of the three cohesive Resistance parties broke in 1947 with the coming of the Cold War. The Fourth Republic lapsed back into the individualism of the Third. In both republics there was, in Aron's words, a "mixed system, in which some candidates owed their election to their personal position in the district or *département,* others to the success of a party." [176] In both republics majority coalitions normally included the centrist Radicals with their tradi-

176. Raymond Aron, *France, Steadfast and Changing: The Fourth to the Fifth Republic* (Cambridge: Harvard University Press, 1960), p. 29.

tion of deputy individualism. In broad political outline the assemblies of the two republics had much in common with the American Congress. Communists aside, deputies had to build and sustain personal followings in order to keep nominations and win elections.[177] Communists again excepted, the parliamentary parties were incohesive in their roll call voting.[178] Assembly committees were as strong and as independent as those in the American Congress.[179]

The result was "assembly coherence." Deputies gave extraordinary time and energy to the supply of particularized benefits to their constituencies.[180] The

177. See Lowell, *Governments and Parties in Europe*, I: 133–36; Philip M. Williams, *Parties in Post-War France: Parties and the Constitution in the Fourth Republic* (New York: Longmans Green and Co., 1958), pp. 154–55, 349, 355. Rosenthal makes a case that Gaullist deputies in the Fourth Republic individually attuned their assembly voting to local coalition needs: ". . . [T]here may be a pure political game of adapting one's position to winning electoral contests. Consideration of what is necessary to win in a constituency may then dictate the deputies' decisions in the Legislature." Howard Rosenthal, "The Electoral Politics of Gaullists in the Fourth French Republic: Ideology or Constituency Interest?" 63 *American Political Science Review* 487 (1969). One difference between French and American legislators is that between one-quarter and one-half of the non-Communist deputies of the Fourth Republic were simultaneously local mayors. Duncan MacRae, Jr., *Parliament, Parties and Society in France, 1946–1958* (New York: St. Martin's, 1967), p. 54.

178. See MacRae, *Parliament, Parties and Society*.

179. See Williams, *Parties in Post-War France*, pp. 234–41.

180. All analysts agree on the point. See, e.g. Williams, *Parties in*

shift from single districts in the Third Republic to proportional representation in the Fourth cut down on "parish-pump politics" but by no means eliminated it.[181] In effect, the shift gave greater electoral value to the servicing of interest groups.[182] Parliamentary committees with organized clienteles clashed with Fourth Republic cabinets on matters like veterans' pensions and teacher salaries.[183] Managing parliamentary business was in itself a formidable task.[184] It was hard to keep budgets in balance.[185] To serve the needs of institutional maintenance there was of course the cabinet but also the Finance Committee, which

---

Post-War France, pp. 205, 252, 257; Lowell, *Governments and Parties in Europe*, I: 220.

181. Williams, *Parties in Post-War France*, p. 349.

182. Ibid., pp. 328–29.

183. Bernard E. Brown, "Pressure Politics in France," p. 715. On committees see also Williams, *Parties in Post-War France*, pp. 240–41.

184. Williams, *Parties in Post-War France*, pp. 207–09. "In refusing to accept a minimum of discipline in the conduct of parliamentary business, the deputies stultify themselves. Their attention is constantly distracted to minor matters instead of being concentrated on the main aspects of policy, which in practice frequently escape from their control." P. 209.

185. Ibid., pp. 252–53, 258–61. "The unwillingness of the deputies to vote for higher taxes was only equalled by their reluctance to accept reductions in expenditure. Ministers and independent observers were in doleful agreement that the members of parliament wanted abstract economies and concrete expenses, a reduction in the total of state expenditures but increases in the individual items." P. 261.

walked the same fine line as the control committees of the American House.[186] As for delay on major policy matters, the French had their own word for it—*immobilisme*. On social policy Thomson argues that parliaments of the Third Republic were exceptionally insensitive to the nonparticularistic needs of the working class.[187]

All this does not add up to a conclusive case that individualistic assemblies cannot govern. With occasional German interruptions the two French republics did after all last for eighty-seven years—not a bad record given the turmoil of the last century. Indeed in the long run a particularistic regime may prove more durable than an efficient bureaucratic state without local roots. And it should be recalled that the French republics, like the American one, were experiments in democracy in ways foreign to elitist party regimes housed in limited monarchies.[188] Citizens rather than

186. "Indeed, the institutional barriers set up by the Assembly against irresponsible expenditure are wholly dependent for their effectiveness on the attitude of the Finance Committee. The position of the latter is therefore a dual one: in some respects it is the most 'governmental' of committees, while at the same time it is the one whose opposition is most dangerous." Ibid., p. 243.

187. David Thomson, *Democracy in France since 1870* (New York: Oxford University Press, 1969), ch. 5. "Thus the experience of the pre-war years bred disillusionment amongst the working classes, and spread the conviction that social reform was, in the existing system and with the prevailing balance of parties, subordinated to the political mechanism of parliamentary manoeuvres." P. 176.

188. A distinction more or less gone from public consciousness.

subjects are needed to appraise the means and ends of policy ventures in individualistic assemblies. Yet the French republics undeniably had problems. There were continual *crises de régime*. In every election during the Fourth Republic at least 40 percent of the electorate voted for antisystem parties.[189] The Napoleonic option was always kept open, and in 1958 it was chosen. The basic problem in an assembly regime is the lack of a clear accountability relation between electorate and officialdom.[190] Voters find it hard to get a handle on government. There is a tendency, dangerous to a regime, for assembly members to be individually esteemed but collectively despised. As in France so in America. Fenno writes, "We do, it appears, love our Congressmen. . . . On the other hand, it seems equally clear that we do not love our Congress," [191]

It was still vivid when Theodore Roosevelt and the French representative had to trail in a black coach behind a dreary line of kings in scarlet coaches at Edward VII's funeral in 1910.

189. Aron, *France, Steadfast and Changing*, p. 19.

190. The popularity ratings of Fourth Republic premiers hovered in the low percentiles, about the same as those recorded by Truman and Nixon in their worst years. The exceptions were readings for Pinay, Mendès-France, and de Gaulle (in his brief role as last premier of the Fourth Republic), who reached for public support outside the parliament. See MacRae, *Parliament, Parties and Society*, pp. 309–10.

191. Fenno, "How Can We Love Our Congressmen?", p. 1. A national Harris survey reported in 1969 turned up these disparate responses: "How would you rate the job which has been done by Congress in 1968—excellent, pretty good, only fair, or poor?"

The tie between Congress and the United States electorate is in some ways a curious and distant one. As table 1 shows, there has been no direct relation in recent years between voter disapproval of congressional performance and voter inclination to deprive incumbents of their seats.

Under the circumstances, keeping Congress afloat for nearly two centuries has been a considerable achievement, and it makes sense to close this essay by speculating briefly on the ways Americans have tried to deal with the problems inherent in congressional rule. A good way to do so is to bring up the American "reform" tradition, which is something to be explained as well as applauded or deplored. By American usage as well as ancient etymology the term *reform* carries a meaning of rationalization—of conferring form or reason where it is lacking. The term is overworked and imprecise, but it can usefully be applied to either or both of the two following kinds of activities: (1) Efforts to impart instrumental rationality to governmental undertakings. In the congressional context this means

---

Excellent or pretty good, 46 percent; fair or poor, 46 percent; not sure, 8 percent. "How would you rate the service your Representative gives in looking after this district in Washington—excellent, pretty good, only fair, or poor?" Excellent or pretty good, 59 percent; fair or poor, 22 percent; not sure, 19 percent. Data supplied by the Institute for Research in Social Science, University of North Carolina.

Table 1. Public Ratings of Congressional Performance Compared with Membership Turnover

| Year | Public Ratings of Congress[a] | | | Number of Incumbents Defeated in Primary or General Elections[b] | | Net Partisan Seat Swing over Previous Election[b] | |
	Positive	Negative	Not Sure	House	Senate	House	Senate
1964	59	33	8	52	3	36D	None
1966	49	42	9	49	4	47R	4R
1968	46	46	8	13	8	5R	6R
1970	26	63	11	22	7	12D	3R

a. Harris survey data supplied by the Institute for Research in Social Science, University of North Carolina. Responses are to a question posed to a national sample at the end of each even-numbered year: "How would you rate the job Congress did in 19**——excellent, pretty good, only fair, or poor?" The first two choices are coded as positive, the last two as negative. Wording of the question has varied slightly over the years.

b. Data taken from *Congressional Quarterly* election reports. Some of the defeats of House members occurred necessarily where redistricting threw two incumbents of the same party into the same district in a primary election or two incumbents of opposite parties into the same district in a November election. There were three throw-in defeats of one kind or the other in 1964, four in 1966, five in 1968, and two in 1970.

attempts to deal with symbolism and delay. (2) Efforts to apply universalistic distributive standards in the activities of government, or, more broadly, to have the government venture forth and impose universalistic distributive standards on society. This last we call "social reform." In the congressional context universalistic standards impinge on particularism[192] or the servicing of the organized. There is no need to decide here what instrumental rationality or universalistic standards "really are." The meanings change from time to time; in effect, the connotative meanings of efficiency and justice change over time. It will suffice here to take a philosophical shortcut and say that reform demands on government are an important class of popular preferences expressed or discussed in the language of efficiency or universalism. Probably every regime generates its own style of reform. The Ameri-

192. This can be true even though the term *universalism* was used earlier to characterize the way congressmen agree among themselves to hand out particularized benefits. Take the example of the impacted areas program. Every congressman who wants an impacted areas subsidy gets one, but there is no overriding rationale for handing out education money this way—or so it is alleged—beyond the political rationale that makes subsidies in visible packets electorally attractive. Hence it is alleged that some school districts and therefore some students profit unjustifiably at the expense of others—an overall violation of universalistic standards. There are no certain answers on questions like these, but there is a language for dealing with them. The Supreme Court makes judgments of this sort in construing the Equal Protection clause of the Fourteenth Amendment.

can style is distinctive, and it fits the contours of American institutions. Its most vigorous component is the "progressive" tradition, with emphases on streamlining government, strengthening executives, rooting out particularism, exposing official complacency and dereliction. Progressivism is largely a middle-class tradition associated only ambiguously with redistributive ventures traveling under the label of "social reform." [193] Indeed the ideological confusion of American reform movements stems from the fact that they have simultaneously in various proportions been quests for efficiency and for justice. In dealing with Congress there are at least four theoretically interesting "reform recourses" to which Americans have turned or thought about turning.

The first and most important recourse has been to

193. It is an interesting question whether social classes differ in their attitudes toward the various American national institutions. Some intriguing data exist for 1960–61. Samples of people with college degrees and people without high school degrees were asked to give their views on congressmen and on high federal government appointees. In the college sample 75 percent gave "favorable portrayals" of the appointees; 65 percent gave "favorable portrayals" of the congressmen. In the other sample the rankings were reversed; the congressmen ran ahead of the appointees by 61 percent to 50 percent. This is not much to go on, but it suggests a middle-class admiration for efficiency putatively found in the executive calling. See M. Kent Jennings, Milton C. Cummings, Jr., and Franklin P. Kilpatrick, "Trusted Leaders: Perceptions of Appointed Federal Officials," 30 *Public Opinion Quarterly* 379–80 (1966).

strengthen the presidential office in the interest of democratic accountability (as in the cities, where mayors have been strengthened over city councils). The logic here is reasonably clear. Since presidents can be held individually accountable for broad policy effects and states of affairs, they are likely to go about their business with a vigorous insistence on instrumental rationality.[194] And both because they are paid for effects and because voter costs of watching their activities are lower, presidents are less likely than congressmen to traffic in particularized benefits or to defer to the organized. So goes the logic. How about the facts? The American record lends a good deal of support to the logic, and indeed it gives a reminder of how often American political controversy has flared between institutions rather than between parties or ideologies.[195] The old tariff issue divided the parties, but it also divided president and Congress.[196] Cleve-

194. John Stuart Mill draws the following distinction between cabinet ministers and assemblies: "To a minister, or the head of an office, it is of more importance what will be thought of his proceedings some time hence, than what is thought of them at the instant: but the assembly, if the cry of the moment goes with it, however hastily raised or artificially stirred up, thinks itself and is thought by everyone to be completely exculpated however disastrous may be the consequences." *Considerations on Representative Government*, pp. 100–01.

195. For an essay on predictable conflict between presidency and Congress see the provocative Willmoore Kendall, "The Two Majorities," 4 *Midwest Journal of Political Science* 317–45 (1960).

196. On the congressional side the pre–New Deal tariff was a truly astonishing political creation. Schattschneider has the best

land's tariff reforms foundered in a Democratic Senate; Taft was ruined by the tariff logrolling of a Republican Senate. Hoover signed the Smoot-Hawley bill, but it was far from what he wanted. Even McKinley supported reciprocity agreements that were given short shrift in a Republican Senate. The tariff was only one pre–New Deal issue. Woodrow Wilson's 1885 work was aptly titled *Congressional Government*—a system in which most of the revenue came in through the tariff and a lot of it went out in veterans' pensions and rivers and harbors projects. Small wonder that Cleveland earned a reputation as a reformer simply by vetoing bills.

The disparities of office have persisted in the modern period. Nixon on the subject of categorical grants sounds like Cleveland on veterans' pensions. Almost every president starting with Coolidge (Johnson and the early Roosevelt are exceptions) has

---

account, and he uses the term "universalization" to characterize the way congressmen agreed among themselves to distribute benefits. Industries followed a policy of "reciprocal non-interference." If there was a duty on a raw material, a "compensatory duty" was levied against finished materials to satisfy manufacturers of the latter. An established duty was regarded as a vested right more or less like an agency's "base" in the appropriations process. Not surprisingly the tariff rates rose higher and higher decade after decade. To dismantle all this in the 1930s was to destroy an elaborate political system. See Schattschneider, *Politics, Pressures, and the Tariff*, pp. 86, 130–31, 135, 144. His summary judgment: "The history of the American tariff is the story of a dubious economic policy turned into a great political success." P. 283.

opposed congressional farm programs. Every president starting with Kennedy has opposed the impacted areas program. Every president starting with Kennedy has had to sell Keynesian economics to a skeptical Hill audience. Presidents surround themselves with definers of efficiency—Louis Brownlow, Herbert Hoover, Robert McNamara, and Roy Ash have been salient among them—provoking clashes with Congress over the organization of the executive branch; Nixon's design for reorganizing the executive branch in 1971 was not far from a carbon copy of Roosevelt's in 1937. Legislative and executive branches attract different personality types—"one oriented to particular relations with persons and another which abstracts from persons to principles." [197] Of the insolence of office there is no shortage; to find a president's man with a contempt for Congress rivaling John Ehrlichman's, one only has to go back to Harry Hopkins. In the area of social reform five of the last six presidents have proposed ambitious redistributive transfer programs and have usually met indifference or hostility on the Hill; Truman, Kennedy, and Nixon, respectively, got nowhere with health insurance, medicare, and family assistance. The presidency is in short a vitally important democratic office which complements the brand of democratic relations offered by Congress.[198] One explanation of

197. Bauer et al., *American Business and Public Policy*, p. 446.
198. Opinion polls assessing presidential performance give a kind of accountability relation that fills in the blanks between

why Congress has maintained its strength reasonably well over the years is that it has sloughed off to the presidency some of the policy problems it is incapable of handling; thus the Bureau of the Budget was lodged in the executive branch in 1921, and the tariff went over to a commission in 1934.[199]

Again there is a French analogy. The French invented the plebiscite, the Americans the presidential election; the latter has proven a more durable electoral connection, and the French have now adopted it.

---

quadrennial election returns. See John E. Mueller, "Presidential Popularity from Truman to Johnson," 64 *American Political Science Review* 18–34 (1970). There is an analogy in Britain where monthly opinion readings on cabinet performance closely match trends in the economy. See C. A. E. Goodhart and R. J. Bhansali, "Political Economy," 18 *Political Studies* 43–106 (1970). In a sense the American Supreme Court is a democratic institution also—an indirectly elected legislature dealing in general rules that Congress is incapable of enacting itself but unwilling to strike down if the Court enacts them. Before the New Deal the rules mostly had to do with domestic free trade, afterward with civil rights and civil liberties.

199. At which time congressional tariff politics shifted largely (but not entirely) from credit claiming to position taking. The modern pattern: "The individual representative can placate a local industry by writing to the Tariff Commission about an escape-clause proceeding or to the Committee on Reciprocity Information when a trade agreement is about to be negotiated. But letters are cheap. He can also make a speech on the floor of Congress or before a trade association. Having done his bit for local industry in this way, he is not necessarily called upon to try to translate local interests into the law of the land." Bauer et al., *American Business and Public Policy*, p. 247.

In fact the French have made the presidency of the Fifth Republic stronger than the American office by severely restricting parliamentary power to amend government bills or propose public expenditures.[200] But to bring up the French tradition is to suggest the difficulties of executive democracy. How democratic can a one-man office be? Leaving aside the problems inherent in centralized decision making—which are serious[201]—there is a simple problem of statistics. A pleasing property of an assembly is that its actions are more or less predictable. Some of its members may turn out to be crooks, incompetents, paranoids, megalomaniacs, or saints, but the proportion will be low and will not change much over time. But no amount of model building can exorcise the fact that a lone president once in office may prove a considerable surprise. An awe-inspiring feature of both Teapot Dome and Watergate is that whole administrations crumbled in ruins. And the presidential temptation to go haring after world glory or a place in the history books is a real one; American foreign policy can come down to a depressing choice between presidential imperialism and congressional symbolism. Moreover,

200. See Philip M. Williams, *The French Parliament: Politics in the Fifth Republic* (New York: Praeger, 1968), pp. 19–20, 66, 81. Some Americans, including Walter Lippmann, have favored the idea of making Congress vote presidential bills up or down within a given time period. See Huntington, "Congressional Responses," p. 30.

201. See Lindblom, *The Intelligence of Democracy.*

when electorates are given a chance to choose national executives, they display a sobering tendency to choose generals. In the public eye what is a military man after all but a package of instrumental rationality? From the Bonapartes through Boulanger and de Gaulle the executive recourse in France (by coup or election) has been military. Weimar Germany supplies the case of Hindenburg. Americans have elected generals when-ever they have been available. It will be recalled that the founder of the Jacksonian tradition was General Jackson—vanquisher of the British and later of the Cherokees. All in all for a democratic people to lodge powers in an elective executive is a risky business. But Americans have taken the risk in order to overcome the policy deficiencies of Congress.

A second American "reform recourse"—more in thought than in action—has been to try to strengthen the political parties either in Congress specifically or in the system generally. The familiar logic of focused accountability has been especially appealing to aca-demics. Beefing up the parties was Woodrow Wilson's first reform nostrum in the years before he discovered the potential of the presidency. There is no need to expound here on the theory of party government.[202] In

202. Downs makes the abstract case for it. Barry discusses the trade-offs between having a "power-concentration" system and a "power-diffusion" system. *Political Argument*, pp. 237–43. In France elites on the left have favored government by party; in the center, government by individualistic assembly; and on the right, govern-

fact the main thrust of reform in twentieth-century
America has been to destroy parties rather than to
strengthen them; progressivism in its heyday was
largely a revolt against the rooted particularism of
American parties at the local level.[203] Within Congress
there does remain as a historical curiosity the venture
in strong party leadership and cohesive party voting
around the turn of the century—especially in the
House between the laying down of the Reed rules in
1890 and the weakening of the Speakership in 1910. In

ment by single-man executive—making for a politics in which
controversy has flourished as often over institutions as over policies.
Most of the arguments against the party model are familiar. Two
perhaps are not. One raises the question whether voters who live in
a system of disciplined parties in fact approve of its arrangements.
Survey evidence on British voters in one locale suggests they would
prefer M.P.'s to be more constituency oriented. See Raymond E.
Wolfinger et al., "Popular Support for the British Party System,"
paper presented to the annual convention of the American
Political Science Association, 1970. Another argument raises the
question whether the abstract assumption of party competitiveness
is necessarily the proper assumption to make. Just about everyone
takes for granted that it is. Writers following Downs have refined
the logic of competition with the tenacity of thirteenth-century
metaphysicians. But why has so little attention been given to
models positing oligopolistic collusion? (Or duopolistic collusion?)
The New York party system, to name one, offers ample material to
flesh out such a case. Some elements of a collusion model appear in
G. William Domhoff, *Fat Cats and Democrats* (Englewood Cliffs,
N.J.: Prentice-Hall, 1972). See also Donald A. Wittman, "Parties
as Utility Maximizers," 67 *American Political Science Review* 490–98
(1973).

203. See Hays, "Political Parties."

its time the bolstering of the Speakership was perceived as a reform. The Reed rules allowed a more expeditious handling of House business.[204] Taussig gives an economist's judgment that the Dingley Tariff Act of 1897 was the better for having been packaged and jammed through by party leaders.[205] But the party experiment was short-lived. Strong Speakers clashed with presidents, and the public accountability relations of the former were inevitably more ambiguous than those of the latter. Speaker Cannon may have been trafficking in a streamlined form of assembly coherence, but, as in the case of the tariff, it was an assembly coherence nonetheless. New reforms overturned the old. Under Taft the progressive insurgents brought into Congress an ethic of member individualism that has since become the norm.[206] Freedom to

204. See Galloway, *History of the House*, pp. 52–53.

205. On its House passage: "In the main, the committee scheme was adopted as it stood, being accepted once and for all as the party measure and passed under the pressure of rigid party discipline. The whole procedure was doubtless not in accord with the theory of legislation after debate and discussion. But it was not without its good side also. It served to concentrate responsibility, to prevent haphazard amendment, to check in some measure the log-rolling and the give-and-take which beset all legislation involving a great variety of interests." Taussig, *Tariff History of the United States*, pp. 326–27.

206. There is an insightful analysis of this progressive ethic in Joseph Cooper, "Progressive Attitudes toward the Proper Role of Committees in the House of Representatives, 1908–1929," unpublished manuscript.

take positions is so firmly established among modern congressmen that something of a revolution would be required to upset it. The current attitude of Democratic incumbents toward the idea of holding midterm national conferences to hammer out party policies is resonantly hostile.[207]

A third recourse, and the favorite of the journalistic profession, is ["exposure."] The logic here is that the diffuseness of American governmental institutions makes it hard for voters to keep track of what incumbent politicians are doing and of the effects of what they are doing. Information costs are extraordinarily high. Hence the muckraking tradition—essentially a persistent effort by journalists and others to reduce information costs.[208] To enlarge the audience on a congressional issue can be to change the outcome. Thus when auto safety arose as an issue in the Eighty-ninth Congress, one ordinarily would have expected the House Commerce Committee to side with the manufacturers. "The reason it did not behave in this fashion can be summarized in a single word: publicity." [209] In this case the publicity was supplied

207. On the controversy over a party "charter" see "Democrats Plan Warily for 1974 National Conference," *Congressional Quarterly Weekly*, June 16, 1973, pp. 1499–1502.

208. Of course a good many reporters enjoy comfortable and symbiótic relations with congressmen. See Matthews, *U.S. Senators*, ch. 9. But others supply a cutting edge of criticism.

209. David Price, *Who Makes the Laws?*, p. 59.

largely by Ralph Nader. In the last decade both the
Nader organization and Common Cause have set up
shop in Washington as publicizers of Capitol Hill
activities.[210] Over the long haul most of the salience-
raising in congressional politics has been the achievement of journalists. Indeed the relation between
reporters and officeholders in American politics is one
of the more important instances of ambition checking
ambition. The logic of exposure has less force in a
system where voters can more clearly judge governments by their effects, and in fact the British have not
sustained an equivalent tradition of exposure.

A fourth and final recourse has been to try to
regulate the deployment of resources in congressional
election campaigns. The chronic effort to regulate
campaign finance is distinctively American; in other
systems where disciplined parties speak for identifiable
social groupings no one much cares where the campaign money comes from. For better or worse almost
all congressional enactments on campaign finance
have been symbolic—bold in theory but haphazardly
drafted and unenforced or unenforceable in practice.
An exception is the Federal Election Campaign Act of
1971, which placed ceilings on radio and television

210. For some interesting theoretical speculation on the formation and functioning of "public interest groups," see Paul A.
Dawson, "On Making Public Policy More Public: The Role of
Public Interest Groups," paper presented at the annual convention
of the American Political Science Association, 1973.

spending by congressional candidates. The law is enforceable because stations keep accurate records of their advertising revenue. Congressional incumbents had an interest in making it enforceable because it protects them from media blitzes by primary or November challengers. One certain yield of Watergate is a new flurry of statutes on campaign finance; whether they will have much effect is difficult to say.

These recourses are as central to American politics as Congress itself. Indeed it is fair to say that in indirect ways two of them—the invoking of the presidency and the tradition of exposure—have contributed as much to the institutional maintenance of Congress as have internal arrangements. And again, keeping individualistic assemblies politically robust is not an easy task. On current trends there are two points worth making. The first is that American national government has recently achieved the complexity of municipal government—an environment in which assemblies have not flourished. The second is that candidates running for Congress have been relying increasingly on position taking; we now have talk-show senators, a House rife with suburbanites, a huge and individualistic California delegation, a reformed New York City delegation. Whether frenetic position takers can make an institution work is a difficult question. No doubt academics and reformers have added to the emphasis on positions by elevating roll call voting as a test of political virtue. Making up ideological indexes is an agreeable enterprise, but from the voter standpoint it ignores at least two other dimensions of considerable importance. There is, or could be, a "particularism-universalism" dimension, gauging the scope of congressmen's activities. And there is, or could be, an "intentions-effects" dimension, gauging the inclination of congressmen to try to accomplish what they say they are in favor of. Appraising congressmen in these ways requires a good deal more information than that supplied in the roll calls, and the Nader profiles of 1972 are probably a response to a felt need for such information. In the long run congressional survival may require institutional maintenance arrangements more sophisticated than the ones that have sufficed in the past. It may be necessary to build in selective incentives to reward members who take an interest in programmatic impact. To do so may be possible in an institution where lifetime careers are the norm. But to do so would be to violate the canons of American legislative politics as we have come to know them.

INDEX

Accountability: of congressmen, 6, 16–17, 38n; in assembly regimes, 164–65; of president, 168–69

Addabbo, Joseph P., 58n

Advertising, as congressional activity: defined and explained, 49–52; and other electoral activities, 73–77; and zero-sum conflict, 82–83

Agriculture programs, 59, 94–95, 115–16, 116n, 121n, 126n, 131, 170–71

Aiken, George D., 104

Albert, Carl, 107

Allocation theory, 142n–43n, 156–58

American Farm Bureau Federation, 66, 116n

American Legion, 66

American Medical Association, 44, 66

Americans for Constitutional Action, 66

Americans for Democratic Action, 37, 66

Anti-Saloon League, 66

Army Engineers, Corps of, 91, 129–30

Aron, Raymond, 160, 164n

Ash, Roy, 171

Assembly coherence, 125–36, 141, 176; in France, 161–63

Auto safety policies, 86, 177

Aydelotte, William O., 20n

Bach, G. L., 127n, 139n

Badillo, Herman, 87

Banfield, Edward C., 23n, 129n, 159n

Barber, James D., 13, 23n

Baring, Walter, 70

Barker, Anthony, 21n

Barone, Michael, 59n, 73

Barrett, William A., 74

Barry, Brian, 87–88, 128n, 130n, 174n

Bauer, Raymond A., 65n, 73, 109n, 148, 171n, 172n

Berlow, Alex, 58n

Bevan, Aneurin, 21

Bhansali, R. J., 172n

Bibby, John F., 67n

Bills, introduction of, 62n–63n

Bismarck, Otto von, 137
Blumler, Jay G., 21*n*
Bolles, Blair, 26*n*
Bolling, Richard, 98*n*
Bonapartism, 164, 174
Bonnen, James T., 126*n*
Boyd, James, 16*n*
Brademas, John, 120
Brandsma, Richard W., 24*n*
Brown, Bernard E., 56*n*, 162*n*
Brown, E. Cary, 131*n*
Brownlow, Louis, 171
Brozen, Yale, 126*n*, 138*n*
Bryce, James, 45*n*, 106*n*
Buchanan, James M., 4, 5*n*, 87, 142*n*
Buckley, James L., 91*n*–92*n*, 119
Budgetary policy, 142–45, 152–58; in France, 162
Bullock, Charles S., III, 14*n*, 38*n*
Business, regulation of, 126*n*, 134–35
Byrd, Robert C., 40, 101
Byrnes, John W., 104

California: state senate, 23*n*; Republicans, 45, 72–73; House delegation, 179
Campaign finance, 26, 39–41, 84; and tax benefits, 57; and committee system, 92–94; strategies, 92*n*–93*n*; reform, 178–79
Campbell, Angus, 28*n*, 144*n*
Campbell, Colin D., 136*n*

Cannon, Joseph G., 26*n*, 176
Careerism in Congress, 14–15, 33, 145–46
Casework, 54–55, 57–59, 84, 108–10
Caves, Richard E., 135*n*
Celler, Emanuel, 104
Chicago: political parties, 23*n*, 25*n*; mayoral endorsements, 42; House delegation, 74–75
Chisholm, Shirley, 87
Christmas tree bills, 57*n*, 155
City councils, 158–60
City machines, 73–74, 121, 159
Civil rights, 67, 76–77, 116, 118, 133, 149. *See also* School bussing
Clapp, Charles L., 26–27, 50*n*, 51*n*, 62*n*, 83*n*, 100*n*, 119*n*, 141*n*
Clark, Joseph, 98*n*–99*n*
Clausen, Aage, 48*n*, 102*n*
Cleveland, Grover, 169–70
Clientelism: and vote mobilization, 115–16; and committees, 131; and symbolism, 134; budgets, 142; in France, 162
Closed rule, 155, 158
Coalition theory, 87–91, 111–21
Coleman, James S., 4*n*, 129*n*
Committees: and credit claiming, 60–61, 87–97; and position taking, 85–87, 97*n*; and particularized benefits, 87–91; and division of labor, 92–

97; subcommittees, 92–97; seniority system, 95–97, 101; and parties, 103–05; Joint Committee on Internal Revenue Taxation, 128–29; in French parliament, 161, 162–63
—House: Appropriations, 1–2, 40*n*, 89, 95*n*, 104*n*, 149–50, 152–54, 156–58; Interstate and Foreign Commerce, 41*n*, 93–94, 177; Public Works, 55*n*, 88, 89–90, 93, 152; Interior and Insular Affairs, 56, 88, 89, 114, 124, 152; Post Office and Civil Service, 61; Foreign Affairs, 73, 74*n*, 97*n*; Banking and Currency, 74, 89, 93; Government Operations, 74*n*; Un-American Activities (Internal Security), 85–86, 147–48; Education and Labor, 86–87, 120, 123–24; Ways and Means, 89, 91, 104, 129, 139*n*, 149–50, 154–58; Agriculture, 95; Judiciary, 104; Armed Services, 122–23; Rules, 149–52, 156–58; Veterans' Affairs, 152
—Senate: Post Office and Civil Service, 61; Commerce, 68*n*, 95*n*; Foreign Relations, 76, 86, 104, 123; Government Operations, 86; Interior and Insular Affairs, 88–89; Appropriations, 89, 152–53; Finance, 89, 129, 139*n*–40*n*, 155; Public Works, 91*n*–92*n*; Armed Services, 122–23
Common Cause, 116, 178
Congratulation-rationalization effect, 38
Congressional Record, 83
Congressional Research Service, 124–25
Connecticut: political parties, 23
Consumer affairs, 68, 126*n*, 134–35
Control committees, 147, 149–58
Cooley, Lenore, 51*n*
Coolidge, Calvin, 170–71
Cooper, Joseph, 176*n*
Cover, Albert, 52*n*
Credit claiming, as congressional activity: defined and explained, 52–61; and other electoral activities, 73–77; and committees, 87–97; ombudsman role, 108–10; and legislating, 121–25; and oversight of administration, 125; regulation of business, 135; transfer programs, 136–37
Crick, Bernard, 21*n*, 22*n*
Crime: policies on, 139
Cummings, Milton, Jr., 149*n*, 168*n*

Davidson, Roger H., 2*n*, 32*n*, 67*n*, 83*n*, 96*n*, 127*n*, 151*n*

Davis, J. Ronnie, 142n
Davis, James W., Jr., 126n
Dawson, Paul A., 178n
Deckard, Barbara, 90n
Defense policy, 86, 122–23, 126n
De Gaulle, Charles, 164n, 174
Delaney, James J., 151
Delay, as policy pattern, 126–27; in France, 163
Delegate role, 32
Democracy: congressional variant, 138–40
Democratic party: unbroken congressional control, 103–04; charter, 177
Depletion allowances, 89n, 156
Dexter, Lewis A., 65n, 73, 109n, 122–23, 148, 171n, 172n
Diggs, Charles C., Jr., 51
Dingley Tariff Act, 176
Dirksen, Everett, 107
Districting: congressional, 105n
Dodd, Thomas, 16n
Dolbeare, Kenneth M., 126n
Domhoff, G. William, 175n
Douglas, Paul H., 15, 44n, 71–72, 82n–83n, 91, 110n, 145n
Downs, Anthony: on parties, 18–19, 23–25, 27, 39n, 53, 174n–75n; on budgets, 143n, 156n
Drew, Elizabeth B., 118n

Eberhart, John C., 150n

Edelman, Murray, 134n
Education programs, 87, 128, 131n, 133, 151, 171. *See also* School bussing
Ehrlichman, John, 171
Eisenhower, Dwight D., 31, 52n, 107, 148
Elections: British, 21–22; to American executive office, 24–25; House partisan swings, 28–32, 34–36, 103; and safe congressmen, 33–37; uncertainty, 35, 47–49; impact of congressmen's activities on, 37–38, 57–59, 69–73; and expected incumbent differential, 39–44; maximizing behavior, 46–48; conservative strategies, 47–49, 67; kinds of activities useful in, 49–77 passim; innovative strategies, 67–69. *See also* Campaign finance; Primary elections; Resources used in election campaigns
Endorsements, 42–43, 44
Epstein, Leon D., 21n, 27n
Erikson, Robert S., 36n, 70
Erskine, Hazel, 131n
Ervin, Sam J., Jr., 107
Evans, Rowland B., 149n
Executive branch: reorganization of, 171
Expected incumbent differential, 39–44
Exposure, politics of, 177–78

Fallon, George H., 93
Family assistance program, 138, 139, 171
Federal Election Campaign Act of 1971, 178–79
Fenno, Richard F., Jr.: study of legislative behavior, 2*n*, 3, 87*n*; goals of congressmen, 16, 87*n*; congressmen in constituencies, 35*n*, 145*n*, 164; House Interior Committee, 56, 89*n*, 90*n*, 114*n*, 124*n*; Post Office committees, 61; Senate Foreign Relations Committee, 76*n*, 86*n*, 123*n*; House Education and Labor Committee, 87, 119–20, 124*n*; Senate Interior Committee, 89*n*; House Appropriations Committee, 89*n*, 90*n*, 104*n*, 149*n*, 152–53; Senate Appropriations Committee, 89*n*, 152–53; Senate Finance Committee, 89*n*; House Foreign Affairs Committee, 97*n*; on congressional leaders, 147; House Ways and Means Committee, 149*n*, 155
Fiellin, Alan, 48*n*
Finney, John W., 123*n*, 142*n*
Fiscal policy, 30–31, 127, 128–29, 130*n*–31*n*, 139, 142–45, 152–54, 156–58, 171; in France, 162
Fisher, Louis, 154*n*
Flood, Daniel J., 51

Fong, Hiram, 34*n*
Foreign policy, 56, 63*n*–64*n*, 107, 139, 173. *See also* Vietnam War; Committees, House, Foreign Affairs; Committees, Senate, Foreign Relations
France: parliamentary parties, 27; interest groups, 56*n*; rule by assembly, 160–64; executive, 172–74; dispute over regime, 174*n*–75*n*
Franking privilege, 52, 84–85
Freeman, A. Myrick, 134*n*
Friedland, Claire, 135*n*
Froman, Lewis A., 100*n*
Fulbright, J. William, 16, 104, 107, 123
Functions of legislatures, 8; expressing public opinion, 106–08; handling constituent complaints, 108–10; legislating and oversight, 110–40

Galli, Georgio, 98*n*
Galloway, George B., 150*n*, 176*n*
Gellhorn, Walter, 108
Germany, West: parliament, 21*n*
Glazer, Sarah, 58*n*
Goldwater, Barry, 69–70
Goodell, Charles, 43, 47, 49
Goodhart, C. A. E., 172*n*
Goodman, Walter, 85*n*, 148*n*
Goss, Carol F., 90*n*

Graham, Frank, 15
Grant programs, 56, 129, 144*n*, 170
Gray, Kenneth J., 58*n*
Great Britain: political parties, 19–22; parliament, 21–22; elections, 34*n*, socialized medicine, 44; support for party system, 175*n*
Green, Edith, 120
Griffin, Robert P., 76*n*, 117
Griffith, Robert, 69*n*, 71
Gun control, 66–67, 131

Haider, Donald, 74*n*
Haley, James A., 58*n*
Harding, Warren G., 130
Harris, Joseph P., 154*n*
Harris, Richard, 66*n*, 84*n*, 93*n*, 94*n*
Hartke, Vance, 57*n*
Harvey, Dennis, 41*n*
Hatfield, Mark O., 117
Haveman, Robert H., 134*n*
Hays, Samuel P., 159*n*, 175*n*
Health insurance, 44, 66, 138, 171
Heath, Edward, 139
Hicks, Louise Day, 87
Hill, Lister, 71
Hinckley, Barbara, 28*n*
Hindenburg, Paul von, 174
Hollings, Ernest, 68
Holmes, Sven, 58*n*
Hoover, Herbert, 170, 171
Hopkins, Harry, 171

Horn, Stephen, 89*n*
House of Representatives, ways different from Senate: advertising activities of members, 52; electoral activities of members, 73; progressive ambitions of members, 75–76; control committees, 149; appropriations policies, 152–53; tax, tariff, and transfer policies, 155
Housing programs, 89, 126*n*, 136
Huckshorn, Robert J., 26*n*
Huitt, Ralph K., 1*n*, 99*n*
Hunter, Marjorie, 68*n*, 148*n*
Huntington, Samuel P., 25*n*, 173*n*

Impoundment, 157
Incumbency: electoral advantages of, 36, 50–52, 84–85, 103, 105
Institutional maintenance: in Congress, 141–58, 179–80; in France, 162–63
Interest groups: in France, 56*n*, 162; postal unions, 61; and roll call voting, 66–67, 130–31; campaign finance, 92–94; and vote mobilizing, 115–16; and clientelism, 131; and congressional leaders, 148; and Rules Committee, 152; and closed rule, 155
Italy: preference voting, 45*n*–

46n; parliamentary parties, 98n; particularism, 130n

Jackson, Andrew, 25n, 174
Jackson, John E., 48n
Javits, Jacob, 83n
Jennings, M. Kent, 168n
Johnson, A. Bruce, 126n
Johnson, Lyndon B.: as president, 31, 107, 127, 138, 170–71; as Senate leader, 76, 149
Jones, Charles O., 95n
Jordan, William A., 135n
Journalists: and reform, 177–78

Katz, Richard S., 34n
Keating, Kenneth, 83n
Kendall, Willmoore, 169n
Kennedy, John F., 15, 127, 151, 171
Key, V. O., Jr., 18n, 24, 64n, 66n, 136n
Keynesian economics, 129n, 130n–31n, 139, 171
Kile, Orville M., 66n
Kilpatrick, Franklin P., 168n
Kingdon, John W., 35, 38, 45n
Koehler, David H., 112n
Koltz, Newton, 58n
Kovenock, David M., 83n, 96n, 127n, 151n
Kramer, Gerald H., 29n, 102n
Kupferstein, Linda M., 74n

Labor unions, 61, 92–94, 120n
Laird, Melvin R., 36n

Landauer, Jerry, 93n
Lane, Robert E., 109–10
Language used in Congress, 138n–39n
LaPalombara, Joseph, 46n
Lardner, George, Jr., 57n
Large, Arlen J., 63n, 139n
Lasswell, Harold D., 17n
Lazarus, Simon, 136n
Lazarus, William, 65n
Leaders, congressional, 26n, 98n, 100–01, 107, 147–49, 175–76
Legislating: as function, 110–40
Legislative behavior, study of, 1–5; sociological approaches, 1–2; economic approaches, 2–7; Fenno on, 87n
Legislative Reference Service, 125n
Lepper, Susan J., 102n
Leuthold, David A., 26n, 42, 43n, 84n
Lieberman, Joseph I., 23n
Lindblom, Charles E., 4, 116, 173n
Lindsay, John, 24
Lippmann, Walter, 173n
Lloyd George, David, 137
Lockard, Duane, 23n
Lodge, Henry Cabot, 127n
Loewenberg, Gerhard, 9, 21n
Logrolling, 87–91, 114, 119n, 121n, 128n
Lowell, A. L., 130n, 161n, 162n
Lowenstein, Allard K., 42

Lowi, Theodore J., 53*n*, 85–86, 126*n*, 131*n*, 136*n*
Lutz, Donald S., 112*n*, 117*n*

Maass, Arthur, 91*n*, 130*n*
McCarthy, Joseph, 69, 71, 86, 107, 149
McCloskey, Paul, 72
McCulloch, William M., 104
Macdonald, Torbert H., 41*n*, 93–94
McGovern, George, 117
McKenzie, R. T., 21*n*
McKinley, William, 170
Mackintosh, John P., 22*n*
McNamara, Robert, 171
MacNeil, Neil, 148*n*
McQuail, Denis, 21*n*
MacRae, Duncan, Jr., 161*n*, 164*n*
Madden, Richard L., 120*n*
Madison, James, 17*n*, 23
Magida, Arthur, 51*n*
Magnuson, Warren, 68, 95*n*
Mahon, George, 154*n*
Mail: congressional, 52, 64, 84–85, 108–09
Mailliard, William S., 72–73
Mancke, Richard, 126*n*
Manley, John F., 3, 89*n*, 128–29, 149*n*, 155*n*, 156*n*
Mansfield, Mike, 141*n*
Marginal congressmen, 28–32, 36*n*
Martin, Joe, 58*n*
Martin, John Bartlow, 159*n*

Masters, Nicholas A., 150*n*
Matthews, Donald R., 2*n*, 48*n*, 58*n*, 63*n*, 75*n*, 82*n*, 83*n*, 96*n*, 177*n*
Matthews, Douglas, 59*n*, 73
Maximizing behavior, 46–48
Mayhew, David R., 36*n*, 103*n*, 105*n*
Mendès-France, Pierre, 164*n*
Meyer, Charles W., 142*n*
Military policy, 86, 122–23, 126*n*
Mill, James, 17*n*
Mill, John Stuart, 8*n*, 106, 169*n*
Miller, Clem, 79
Miller, Norman C., 36*n*, 52*n*, 95*n*
Miller, Warren E., 28*n*, 38*n*, 50*n*
Mills, Wilbur D., 104, 139*n*
Minimum wage, 71–72, 126*n*, 138
Minimum winning coalitions, 111–15
Mr. Smith Goes to Washington, 141*n*
Mize, Chester L., 35
Mobilizing activity in Congress, 111–21
Money: as electoral resource. *See* Campaign finance
Monroney, A. S. Mike, 125*n*
Mooney, Booth, 148*n*
Moynihan, Daniel P., 139*n*–40*n*
Muckraking, 177–78
Mudd, Roger, 116

Mueller, Dennis C., 15*n*
Mueller, John E., 172*n*
Murphy, James T., 55*n*, 89*n*, 90, 91*n*
Murphy, Jerome T., 133*n*
Murray, Richard W., 112*n*, 117*n*

Nader, Ralph, 61, 177–78
Namier, Lewis, 27
National Rifle Association, 66–67, 131
Neustadt, Richard E., 20*n*, 43
New York City: mayoralty elections, 24; House delegation, 74, 179
Niemi, Donald, 3*n*
Niskanen, William A., 2, 4, 122*n*, 126*n*, 142*n*–43*n*
Nixon, Richard M., 24, 73, 107, 138, 139, 157, 164*n*, 170, 171
Noggle, Burl, 107*n*
Noll, Roger, 135*n*
Nominating systems: British, 20; American, 25–26; conventions in nineteenth century, 45*n*; Italian preference voting, 45*n*–46*n*; French, 161. *See also* Primary elections
Nonidez, Cynthia T., 32*n*
Novak, Robert, 149*n*

Obey, David R., 36*n*
Odegard, Peter H., 66*n*
Offices of congressmen, 84–85, 108

O'Leary, Michael K., 83*n*, 96*n*, 127*n*, 151*n*
Olson, David M., 32*n*
Olson, Kenneth G., 55*n*
Olson, Mancur, Jr., 130*n*, 145–46
Ombudsman role, 108–10
O'Neill, Thomas P., 148*n*
Opposition: strategies of, 30–31; role of, 106–07
Ornstein, Norman J., 97*n*
Ostrogorski, Moisei, 26*n*
Oversight of administration: as function, 110–40

Pareto optimality, 7
Paris, John, 41*n*
Particularism: allocation rules, 90; and position taking, 91; as policy pattern, 127–30; and symbolism, 134; and budgets, 142; and congressional leaders, 148; Rules Committee, 151–52; House Appropriations Committee, 152–54; Ways and Means Committee, 154–56; in cities, 159; and reform, 167–68; president and Congress, 169–72
Particularized benefits: House Appropriations Committee, 40*n*; defined, 53–54; examples, 54–57; electoral impact, 57–59; and information costs, 60; and city machines, 73–

Particularized benefits (cont.)
74; and committees, 87–91;
allocation rules, 90–91; om-
budsman role, 108–10; and
vote mobilizing, 114; and
logrolling, 119n; military pol-
icy, 122–23; and particular-
ism, 127–30; and transfer
programs, 136–37; in France,
161
Passell, Peter, 157n
Payne, James L., 13n
Peabody, Robert L., 100n, 149n
Pearson, James B., 41
Pechman, Joseph A., 144n
Pepper, Claude, 71
Perkins, Carl, 120
Perry, James M., 76n
Pinay, Antoine, 164n
Pincus, Walter, 93n
Plott, Charles R., 89n, 90n
Policy effects, study of, 126n
Political parties: in Downsian
model, 18–19; British, 19–22;
American, 22–25; in Con-
necticut, 23; in Chicago, 23n;
organizations in primaries,
25–26; and electoral re-
sources, 26–27; and cabinet
regimes, 27; in Italian parlia-
ment, 98n; French, 160–61;
as reform recourse, 174–77;
Democratic party charter,
177
—congressional, 97–105; and
zero-sum politics, 97–99, 105;

minority party, 97, 102–05;
programs, 98–99; and position taking, 99–102; leaders,
100–01; whips, 100; lack of
third parties, 101–02; party
voting, 102–03; and com-
mittees, 103–05; and role of
opposition, 106–07; at turn
of century, 175–76
Pollution policies, 134
Polsby, Nelson W., 14n, 88n, 100n
Pool, Ithiel de Sola, 65n, 73,
109n, 148, 171n, 172n
Position taking, as congressional activity: defined and
explained, 61–73; and other
electoral activities, 73–77;
and zero-sum conflict, 83;
and committees, 85–87, 97n;
and particularized benefits,
91; and parties, 99–102; and
public opinion, 106–08; and
vote mobilizing, 114–19; electoral demand for, 121, 179;
and legislating, 121–25; and
symbolism, 132–36; policy
means and ends, 138–40; and
modern tariff, 172n
Powell, Adam Clayton, 120
Powell, Enoch, 21
Prandi, Alfonso, 98n
Presidency: and partisan electoral swings, 28–32; influence in Congress, 43; senators
running for, 75–76; and particularism, 128; and veterans'

bonuses, 130; and transfer programs, 137–38; as reform recourse, 168–74; polls on, 171n–72n

Prewitt, Kenneth, 14n

Price, David, 68n, 86n, 95n, 177n

Price, H. Douglas, 7n, 14n

Primary elections, 25–26, 32–33, 35, 41, 45, 46–49, 102n

Professionalization of legislatures, 7

Progressive ambitions of congressmen, 75–76

Progressivism, 168, 175, 176

Prohibition, 133, 136

Proxmire, William, 86

Public assistance programs, 137

Public finance: study of, 4–5, 6, 122n, 142n–43n, 153, 156n

Public opinion: congressional polls, 45; expression of, 106–08; on Congress, 127, 164n, 165, 166, 168n; on French leaders, 164n; on presidents, 171n–72n

Rabushka, Alvin, 126n

Rae, Douglas, 102n

Ranney, Austin, 20n

Ratings of congressmen, 66, 179–80

Rawls, John, 7, 156n

Rayburn, Sam, 148, 149

Reed rules, 175–76

Reeves, Richard, 92n

Reform: seniority system, 96–97; in cities, 158–59; as American tradition, 165–68; invoking of presidency, 168–74; of political parties, 174–77; Democratic party charter, 177; exposure, 177–78; campaign finance, 178–79

Regulation of business, 126n, 134–35

Representative assembly: definition of, 8–9

Republican party: minority congressional status, 103–04

Research: and legislating, 124–25

Resources used in election campaigns, 26–27, 39–44; British elections, 21

Responsible legislators, 150

Revenue policy, 56–57, 89, 91, 127, 128–29, 143n, 144–45, 154–58

Ribicoff, Abraham, 86

Riker, William H., 3, 111–12, 114n

Ripley, Randall B., 100n–01n

Robinson, James A., 151n, 152n

Roll call voting: in Britain, 20; support of president, 29–30; reliance on cues, 48; and position taking, 61, 65–67; impact on elections, 69–73; on public works, 91n; and congressional parties, 99–103; mobilizing activity, 111–21;

Roll call voting (continued)
  in state legislatures, 112n,
  117n; and interest groups,
  130–31; in France, 161; at
  turn of century, 175–76;
  rating of congressmen, 179–
  80
Roosevelt, Franklin D., 107,
  130, 137–38, 170–71
Rosenbaum, David E., 64n
Rosenberg, Nathan, 5n
Rosenthal, Howard, 161n
Ross, Leonard, 136n, 157n
Rothchild, John, 121n
Rovere, Richard, 69n
Roybal, Edward R., 64–65
Rules suspension, 148
Rush, Michael, 21n
Russell, Richard, 147n

Safe congressmen, 33–37
Saxbe, William B., 11
Schattschneider, E. E., 18n,
  56n, 91n, 130n, 169n–70n
Scher, Seymour, 3, 125n, 135n
Schlesinger, Joseph A., 75n
Schneier, Edward V., 102n,
  103n
Schoenberger, Robert A., 69
School bussing, 71, 99, 115, 117
Schultze, Charles L., 123n, 126n
Scott, Helen A., 126n
Scott, Hugh, 157n
Seidman, Harold, 131n–32n,
  134n
Selective incentives, 146, 180

Senate, ways different from
  House. *See* House of Rep-
  resentatives, ways different
  from Senate
Seniority system, 95–97, 101,
  101n–02n
Sesser, Stanford N., 67n
Shanahan, Eileen, 91n
Sherrill, Robert, 40n, 101n
Shils, Edward A., 86n
Shipley, George E., 51
Showdown votes, 67
Shriver, Garner E., 40n
Smith, Frank E., 16n
Snowiss, Leo M., 25n, 75n
Social class: and congressional
  mail, 108–09; and percep-
  tions of government, 168n
Social security, 136–38, 154–55
Sokolow, Alvin D., 24n
Southern Manifesto, 63, 71
Speeches by congressmen, 63–
  65
Spencer, Robert C., 26n
State legislatures, 23, 112n, 117n
Steiner, Gilbert Y., 137n
Stern, Philip M., 39n, 89n
Sterne, Richard S., 126n
Stigler, George J., 135n
Stimson, James A., 48n
Stokes, Donald E., 22n, 28n,
  30n, 34n, 38n, 50n, 62n
Subcommittees, 94–97
Sullivan, Joseph W., 105n
Supporting coalition, 45, 103
Surrey, Stanley S., 57n, 89n

Symbolism: Buckley on, 119; as policy pattern, 132–36; and House Rules Committee, 152; and House Appropriations Committee, 153; as waste, 156n; and reform, 165, 167–68

Szita, Ellen, 40n, 51n

Tacheron, Donald G., 50n, 64n

Taft, William Howard, 170, 176

Talmadge, Herman E., 68n

Tariff policy: pre-New Deal, 55–56, 88n, 91n, 104n, 129, 169–70, 176; allocation rules, 91n; concern with effects, 144; post-New Deal, 148, 154–56, 172

Taussig, F. W., 104n, 176

Tax policy, 56–57, 89, 91, 127, 128–29, 143n, 144–45, 154–58

Teapot Dome, 107, 173

Televising of House hearings, 148

Thompson, Frank, Jr., 58–59

Thomson, David, 163

Thurmond, Strom, 76–77

Tiernan, Robert O., 41n

Transfer programs, 136–38, 154–55, 171. *See also* Family assistance program; Veterans' benefits

Truman, David B., 30n, 121n

Truman, Harry S., 107, 130n, 139, 164n

Tufte, Edward R., 103n–04n

Tullock, Gordon, 4, 87, 132n, 142n

Turner, Julius, 102n, 103n

Turnover in congressional membership, 13–15, 33n, 75–76, 165, 166

Tydings, Joseph, 67n

Tydings, Millard, 71n

Udall, Morris K., 50n, 64n, 85n

Ujifusa, Grant, 59n, 73

Uncertainty, in elections, 47–49

Urban, Richard, 126n

Vardaman, James K., 64

Veterans' benefits, 66, 128, 130, 137, 148, 170

Vietnam War, 61, 64, 65, 73, 107, 117, 120–21, 138

Wahlke, John C., 2n

Walsh, Thomas J., 107

Waste, 153–54, 156

Watergate, 107, 173, 179

Wheare, K. C., 106n

Wheeler, Burton D., 107

Whips, party, 100

White, Leonard D., 154n

White, Morton, 140

Whitten, Jamie, 95n, 158n

Wieck, Paul R., 101n

Wilcox, Walter, 51n

Wildavsky, Aaron, 3, 126n

Williams, Philip M., 161n, 162n, 163n, 173n

Wilson, James Q., 139*n*, 159*n*

Wilson, Woodrow, 18*n*, 83*n*, 98,
  143*n*, 153*n*, 170, 174

Wittman, Donald A., 175*n*

Wolfinger, Raymond E., 175*n*

Young, John, 58*n*

Zandman, Anne, 51*n*

Zero-sum conflict in Congress,
  82–83, 97–99, 105, 111–15